". . . the most exciting—and most inadequately reported—direction in psychology and education today. The methods he offers can help both professionals and laymen alike. They work."

—George Leonard
Esalen Institute

"A superb statement—unpretentious, crystal clear and vivid. It should help all psychotherapists to break out of the straitjacket of purely verbal approaches."

—Jerome Frank, M.D.
Professor of Psychiatry
Johns Hopkins University

". . . an original, lively, challenging formula for relaxing rigid personalities—and others."

—Gordon Allport, Ph.D.
late Professor of Psychology
Harvard University

"Every now and then something truly unique and outstanding is admitted to the literature of the therapeutic world . . . With Joy, we find a whole new vista of methods, ways and means to tap the areas of conflict that engulf a human being and create misery, unhappiness, and physical ailments. . . . This is truly something new, and of great benefit to the problems that our nation and the world today suffer."

—J. Dudley Chapman, D.O.
Editor-in-Chief
The Osteopathic Physician

JOY is ". . . controversial, **seductive,** outrageous in aspiration and exciting in attainment. It is disrepectful of the protective boundaries among professional disciplines and crafts. It breaks new ground, far outstrips whatever research is available, takes from many diverse fields, and enriches these fields in return. Crossfertilization occurs with little concern for paternity of ideas or method."

—Jack R. Gibb
Contemporary Psychology

JOY

JOY Expanding Human Awareness

by William C. Schutz

Grove Press, Inc., New York

Library of Congress Catalog Card Number: 67-27879

First Evergreen Black Cat Edition, 1969
Fifth Printing

Manufactured in the United States of America

To Laurie, Caleb, Ethan—*pure joy*

... well, most of the time

Contents

7

Prologue

I suppose it all started when Ethan was born. The idea of writing about joy had been rummaging around for some time, but he crystallized the feelings behind the rummaging. He emerged via natural childbirth, Lamaze method, and I was there. I saw him enter the world, get turned upside down, cry a little and then stop, get cleaned off, wrapped up, and put into my arms.

As I looked at him, he was very quiet and very curious. He lay quite still, concentrating on the "blooming, buzzing confusion," apparently entranced. For an hour we held him, and he was warm and close and peaceful. I even found myself trying to explain what he was getting into— and he listened carefully. I kept thinking that this might be the most important hour of his life. What a way to begin, by giving joy to parents!

The joy continues. When Ethan smiles, every cell of his body smiles, including his turned-up toes. When he is unhappy, he is thoroughly unhappy, all over. When he is interested in a new object, only he and the object exist. He touches it, tastes it, smells it, puts it in things, puts things in it, gives it to people, takes it from people, looks at it from far and from near. The total absorption is beautiful to watch.

And his pleasure now, during his first fifteen

months, is mainly physical—being thrown up in the air, sliding off the refrigerator into his father's arms, being tickled and hugged, having his cheeks chewed, his behind munched, his face caressed, rubbing his cheek against another's cheek. And he touches. It's hard to match the feeling of his little finger exploring my teeth way inside my mouth while his face has that curious, intent look.

And on it goes. He is joyful and he gives joy. He wakes up each morning eager for new adventure. Maybe today it will be a piece of string, or the toilet plunger, or the telephone, or pots and pans, or—more rarely—a new toy.

Ethan is joy. He enjoys each aspect of his life with his whole being. He gives joy to those near him. His joy is contagious.

But will something happen to Ethan as it does to us all? Where will his joy go? In most of us it becomes depleted, distorted, contorted. Guilt and fear begin to defile it. Somehow the joy of Ethan goes, never to fully return.

Perhaps we can recapture some joy, regain some of the body-pleasures, share again the joy with other people that once was possible. This book strives to make an inroad in that direction, by presenting some thoughts and methods for attaining more joy. It is an attempt to provide a framework for various approaches to joy and the development of the human potential. These methods come from psychotherapy ("making sick people well"); human-relations training ("making well people better"); from the arts, especially dance and drama; from Eastern philosophy and religion; and from existential philosophy. My conviction is that the time is right for most of these methods to be pre-

sented to the general public. Too often we are too
precious with these techniques. Several methods
from psychotherapy, for example, could easily be
used profitably in everyday life without the need
for the therapist's office or supervision.

A cornerstone of this approach is honesty and
openness. This may seem simple, but it's not.
Training people to be direct and not devious, to
express their feelings honestly—this is difficult
and often fraught with risk, but enormously rewarding. Directness deepens and enriches relationships, and opens up feelings of warmth and closeness that are rare in most of our experiences. As
the methods are described, you will see how essential an honest interaction is to the achievement
of human potential and of joy.

This approach is in many ways against our culture. We have quite a few words for hypocrisy, like
tact, diplomacy, discretion—concepts which are
dominant in public life, and which usually go un-
challenged. Sometimes they lead to spectacular
failure, as in the current "credibility gap" that is
eroding a political administration, or in the situation that has led to youth's demand that we "tell
it like it is." Much more openness and candor, I
believe, leads to much more joy for all.

The methods presented in the book involve
doing something, not just talking. In this sense
they often diverge from more traditional psychotherapy and, I believe, raise several important
issues for traditional psychotherapy. Talking is
usually good for intellectual understanding of personal experience, but it is often not as effective
for helping a person to *experience*—to feel. Combining the non-verbal with the verbal seems to

create a much more powerful tool for cultivating human growth.

The current interest in LSD and other psychedelic drugs has a relation to the joy techniques. The aims are similar—to make the experience of life more vital. The joy methods attempt to achieve this without drugs. How similar the experiences are I don't know personally, but several people who have experienced both feel there are some close similarities.

Now some words of caution. The experiences described here are in no sense panaceas. Often the examples report remarkable success, and as far as can be determined they are quite accurate. But usually the examples describe the most successful instances of the method. There are other occasions where the technique was of little value.

The fact that no one method works well for everyone creates a need for a multiplicity of methods. By having a wide variety of approaches, it is more likely that each person can find one or more techniques that he can work with profitably. Also, each person is at a different point in his psychological development. For one person, one technique might be just what he needs to enter into a new, better phase of life. For another, it might just start a series of events which then need to be followed up by more similar experiences. Some techniques require cautions. Where these cautions are stated, they should be adhered to, so that maximum value can be obtained from the techniques.

The future is exciting. The pursuit of joy is exciting. The time is now. We'd better hurry. The culture is already getting to him—Ethan looks as if he is beginning to feel frightened and guilty.

To dream the impossible dream
To fight the unbeatable foe
To bear with unbearable sorrow
To run where the brave dare not go
To right the unrightable wrong
To be better far than you are
To try when your arms are too weary
To reach the unreachable star
This is my quest . . .

—Don Quixote in *Man of La Mancha*

JOY

1 · The Quest

If there is one statement true of every living person it must be this: he hasn't achieved his full potential. The latent abilities, hidden talents, and undeveloped capacities for excellence and pleasure are legion. The consequences of this universal fate are many. Observers frequently refer to the human potential as our largest untapped natural resource. Increasing leisure time underlines the significance of unused potential. And perhaps most important of all, the unexpressed robs us of pleasure and joy in living—it prevents us from "reaching the unreachable star."

The theme of this book is joy. The theories and methods presented here are aimed at achieving joy. Joy is the feeling that comes from the fulfillment of one's potential. Fulfillment brings to an individual the feeling that he can cope with his environment; the sense of confidence in himself as a significant, competent, lovable person who is capable of handling situations as they arise, able to use fully his own capacities, and free to express his feelings. Joy requires a vital, alive body, self-contentment, productive and satisfying relations with others, and a successful relation to society.

Obstacles to realizing this potential come from everywhere. The methods used to organize social institutions frequently squelch creativity and impose mediocrity. Society seems to place a premium on relationships featuring hypocrisy and superficiality—relationships that are tolerated rather than sources of happiness. Child-rearing practices, sexual attitudes, much religious dogma, attitudes toward material achievement, confusion about maleness and femaleness—all coalesce to make it difficult for an individual to learn to know himself, to like himself, to become acquainted with his real feelings and desires, and to learn to use himself effectively and joyously.

Our bodies, too, can inhibit the development of joy. Poor physical condition, physical trauma, and emotional problems (converted into physical ailments, weakness, and malformations) limit a person's capacity for full realization. A pained, tired, deadened, or unfeeling body cannot experience itself fully and cannot hold the feelings required for optimal fulfillment of the individual.

In recent decades, many investigators have been working on theories and methods for developing the human potential. As yet, these practitioners are not united behind one coherent approach, but each works at a vitally important element of the problem. From organizations to interpersonal relations to physical health to creativity, workers are exploring ways to develop the human potential.

Attempts at integration of these approaches are sparse and increasingly needed. *Look* magazine's recent issue on California (June 28, 1966) was a fine journalistic attempt to capture the essence of the human-potentiality movement by concentrating on the state in which the greatest activity has occurred. The present effort offers a framework for organizing and comprehending these approaches, along with a description of various methods.

The underlying philosophy behind the human-potential thrust is that of openness and honesty. A man must be willing to let himself be known to himself and to others. He must express and explore his feelings and open up areas long dormant and possibly painful, with the faith that in the long run the pain will give way to a release of vast potential for creativity and joy. This is an exhilarating and frightening prospect, one which is often accompanied by agony, but which usually leads to ecstasy.

To explore the areas needed for the full development of the human potential, it is helpful to know what a man who has developed his full potential—let us call him a fully realized man—looks like. What are the various pressures that can prevent him from realizing this potential? And where, therefore, must methods be devised for overcoming inhibitions facilitating its development? Man is a biological, psychological, and social animal and his joy comes from these sources.

To begin with, man is a biological organism. His first point of inhibition is in his physical structure. If a man is sickly and weak, if his energy is low or his vital functions are impaired, it is unlikely that he can function at his utmost. The first area of "realization" is the physical structure. Bodily joy comes not simply from an athletic body but from one that functions smoothly, gracefully, without unnecessary strain; a body in which the joints move easily, the muscles are toned, the blood flows vigorously, the breathing is deep and full, food is digested well, the sexual apparatus is in good order, and the nervous system works effectively. This level of approach will be called The Body (Chapter 2).

Joy also arises from the full development of personal functioning. The parts of the body may be taught and trained, exercised and sharpened. The senses may be made more acute to discriminate smells and sights. Strength and stamina can be increased in the muscles. Sensory awareness and appreciation can be awakened so that more sensitivity to bodily feelings and natural events can be developed. Motor control can be cultivated so that development of mechanical and artistic skills result, and coordination and dexterity improve. The nervous system may be developed through study and the acquisition of knowledge and experience. Logical thinking and the creative potential can be nurtured and brought to fruition. Bodily functions controlling the emotions can also be developed. Awareness of emotions, appropriate expression of feelings (and their relation to other functions such as thinking and action) can be trained. This approach will be called Personal Functioning (Chapter 3).

Thus far our "realized" man has acquired a finely tuned body, and has developed it to its full integrated functioning. If he is to develop further, he must be able to relate to other people in order to achieve the most joy. Since ours is a communal culture, this means functioning in such a way that human interaction is rewarding for all concerned. How to describe techniques for successfully relating to others is a difficult task, though a subject on which several authors have offered solutions. I will use an approach that I proposed in an earlier publication.[1]

This theory asserts that our needs from and toward other people are three: *inclusion, control,* and *affection.* We achieve interpersonal joy when we find a satisfying, flexible balance in each of these areas between ourselves and other people. *Inclusion* refers to the need to be with people and to be alone. The effort in inclusion is to have enough contact to avoid loneliness and enjoy people; enough aloneness to avoid enmeshment and enjoy solitude. The fully realized man can feel comfortable and joyful both with and without people, and knows with how much of each—and when—he functions best. In the area of *control* the effort is to achieve enough influence so that a man can determine his future to the degree that he finds most comfortable, and to relinquish enough control so that he is able to lean on others to teach, guide, support, and at times to take some responsibility from him. The fully realized man is capable of either leading or following as appropriate, and

------

[1] The theory was originally presented in a book published by Holt, Rinehart in 1958 under the title *FIRO: A Three Dimensional Theory of Interpersonal Behavior.* The book has since been reprinted in paperback with the new title *The Interpersonal Underworld,* by Science and Behavior Books, 577 College Avenue, Palo Alto, California. There are several questionnaires available for testing many of the ideas derived from the FIRO theory. These are published by Consulting Psychologists Press, at the same Palo Alto address.

of knowing where he personally feels most comfortable. In *affection* the effort is to avoid being engulfed in emotional entanglement (not being free to relate without a deep involvement), but also to avoid having too little affection and a bleak, sterile life without love, warmth, tenderness, and someone to confide in. The fully realized man is aware of his needs, and functions effectively not only in close, emotionally involving situations, but also in those of lesser intensity. As in the other two areas, he is able to both give and take, comfortably and joyfully. This approach to the human potential shall be called Interpersonal Relations (Chapter 4).

One other level must be dealt with before the fully realized man is complete. Assume now that he has a good body structure, functioning well, and he relates optimally with the people of his life. But he functions within a society, and his development cannot be completed without the support of the society. If the society is repressive, he cannot develop fully. If social institutions are destructive, he cannot grow. If family life is constricting, if work is dehumanizing, if laws are humiliating, if norms are intolerable, if bigotry and prejudice are the bases of human functioning, then our fully realized man is in deep trouble. Joy at the level of organization comes when society and culture are supporting and enhancing to self-realization. Approaches at this level will be called Organizational Relations (Chapter 5).

This, then, is our framework. Joy is developed through the levels of body structure, personal functioning, interpersonal relations, and organizational relations. Joy is the feeling that comes when one realizes his potential for feeling, for having inner freedom and openness, for full expression of himself, for being able to do whatever he is capable of, and for having satisfying relations with others and with society.

How is joy attained? A large part of the effort, unfortunately, must go into undoing. Guilt, shame, embarrassment, or fear of punishment, failure, success, retribution—all must be overcome. Obstacles to release must be surmounted. Destructive and blocking behavior, thoughts, and feelings must be altered. Talents and abilities must be developed and trained. It sounds overwhelming, but there is cause for optimism. Much work is now being done at all levels. The following pages will present these levels in somewhat more detail and describe some of the exciting techniques now being used to help realize the human potential.

I have learned the large majority of these methods from other people. The methods have in common the fact that I have experienced them, in all cases used them in my own work with others, and found them extraordinarily effective. Most can be used by the layman interested in exploring himself, his relation to others, his relation to society, and his own creativity. Some require more professional handling. Where this is so, it is noted.

Most of the examples used to illustrate the techniques occurred in encounter groups.[2] An encounter group is usually comprised of six to twelve

[2] L. Bradford, J. Gibb, and K. Benne, *T-group Theory and Laboratory Method*, New York, Wiley, 1964; and E. Schein and W. Bennis, *Personal and Organizational Change Through Group Methods*, New York, Wiley, 1965.

people who meet together for the primary purpose of personal growth. The members of the group are usually not emotionally "sick" in the sense of being psychotic or seriously neurotic. Typically, they are the normals and normal neurotics that make up the bulk of our population.

An encounter group has no preset agenda. Instead, it uses the feelings and interaction of group members as the focus of attention. The process of achieving personal growth begins with the exploration of feelings within the group and proceeds to wherever the group members take it. A strong effort is made to create an atmosphere of openness and honesty in communicating with each other. Ordinarily, a strong feeling of group solidarity develops and group members are able to use each other very profitably.

The leader of the group is generally someone with a strong academic background in the social sciences who has had special training in the conduct of encounter groups. Often this person also has some experience in group therapy as well. The leader's purpose is to do whatever is required to help the group members attain their growth goals; he may be silent, supportive, challenging, informative, tough, disclosing, tender, aggressive, insightful, or whatever seems to move the group along. Naturally, leader behavior varies greatly with the personality of the trainer. In the groups from which the examples given here were drawn, I served as the group leader, and references to Bill or, in one case, Dr. Schutz, refer to me in this role.

Encounter groups are frequently offered in laboratory or workshop settings where several groups function simultaneously, each with its own group leader. This arrangement allows for additional activities involving events between groups, and also helps create a feeling of community that can be very supportive. Typically, these workshops last for one or two weeks. In some of the examples presented below, references are made to the "laboratory" or the "workshop."

The terms "T-group" (T for training), and "sensitivity training group" are commonly used for this type of group. In general they are used synonymously with "encounter group." If there is any distinction, it may be that T-group, the original term used by the National Training Laboratories (see note 3), refers to a number of different types of groups including those oriented more toward organizational dynamics. "Encounter group" is a term more in favor on the West Coast and usually refers more specifically to groups oriented toward individual growth and development. "Sensitivity training" is used in both senses. Places where encounter groups are offered are listed on the following page.

Let us begin the quest at the basic biological level of the body.

There are several organizations where encounter groups or T-groups are used extensively. Some of the most active are:

Esalen Institute
Big Sur, Calif. 93920
For information write:
Esalen Institute
P.O. Box 31389
San Francisco, Calif. 94131
(415) 431–8771
Director: Michael Murphy

National Training
Laboratories
1201 16th Street N.W.
Washington, D.C. 20036
(202) 234–4848
Director: Leland Bradford

Kairos
Wishing Well Hotel
Rancho Sante Fe, Calif.
90670
(714) 756–1123
Director: Robert Driver

Anthos
P.O. Box 1028
New York, N.Y. 10022
(212) 988–9646
Director: Robert Kriegel

Oasis
1439 Michigan Avenue
Chicago, Ill. 60605
(312) 922–8294
Director: Robert Shapiro

Hara
7322 Blairview
Dallas, Texas 75230
(214) 363–7581
Director: Ben Goodwin

Evergreen Institute
2244 South Albion
Denver, Colo. 80222
(303) 756–4129
Director: Carl Hollander

Associates For Human
Resources
387 Sudbury Road
Concord, Mass. 01742
(617) 369–7810
Director: Jack Marvin

Bucks County Seminar
House
Erwinna, Pa. 18920
(215) 294–9400
Director: Grenville Moat

Espiritu
1214 Miramar
Houston, Texas 77006
(713) 528–3301
Director: Leland Johnson

2 · The Body

After many years of being all but ignored, the importance of body-functioning to emotional states is becoming recognized more widely and applied to growth-producing situations. A particularly fascinating discovery is the fruitfulness of certain language which, in describing emotional and behavioral states, translates almost literally into terms used to describe bodily states and functions. This translation has a profound impact on methods of dealing effectively with emotional states. A method for helping a person act out and deal with the sense of being immobilized by others, for example, is to put him in a tight circle of people and ask him to try to break out, physically. The method is based on the transformation of his *emotional* feeling of immobilization into the experience of being *physically* immobilized, to allow him the opportunity to break what he feels are unbreakable bonds. . . . But this is getting ahead of our story.

Implicit general recognition of the close connection between the emotional and the physical is evident in the verbal idioms that have developed in social interaction. Feelings and behavior are expressed in terms of all parts of the body, of body-movement, and of bodily functions. Following is a partial list of some of the terms in common

27

usage that describe behavior and feelings in bodily terms:

lost your head	shoulder a burden
heads up	get it off your chest
sorehead	lot of gall
save face	no guts
two-faced	get off my back
face up	no backbone
chin up	my aching back
get in your hair	spine-tingling
hair-raising	twist your arm
grit your teeth	open arms
skin of your teeth	put the finger on
give your eyeteeth	tight-fisted
pain in the neck	palm off
nose out of joint	give him a hand
nosey	back of your head
hard-nosed	get out of hand
bend your ear	knuckle down
ear to the ground	knuckle under
butterflies in the stomach	elbow your way
can't stomach it	get a leg up
yellow belly	watery knees
bleeding heart	stand on your own feet
broken-hearted	put your toe in water
heart in your throat	tight ass
heartless	no balls
lily-livered	you have your nerve
vent your spleen	gets under the skin
stiff upper lip	thin-skinned
bare your teeth	blood-curdling
sink your teeth into	pissed off
eyebrow lifting	choke up
sweat of your brow	kiss off

catch your eye	keep in touch
starry-eyed	shrug it off
big mouth	get a kick out of it
cheeky	got a kick coming
turn the other cheek	itching to do it
shoulder to the wheel	sucker

Supporting the recognition in everyday life of the close connection between bodily and emotional and mental states, there is a growing volume of theoretical work describing these connections and the way they develop and manifest themselves.

Psychosomatic medicine has made a strong case for the fact that emotional states affect the body. More recently, the opposite view has also been developed—that body-organization and physiology affect the feelings—a view called "somatopsychic." Psychological attitudes affect body-posture and functioning, and this body-formation then has a strong influence on subsequent feelings. In the theoretical work underlying a new technique, Ida Rolf[1] states it this way:

> An individual experiencing temporary fear, grief, or anger, all too often carries his body in an attitude which the world recognizes as the outward manifestation of that particular emotion. If he persists in this dramatization or consistently re-establishes it, thus forming what is ordinarily referred to as a "habit pattern," the muscular arrangement becomes set. Materially

---

[1] Ida Rolf, "Structural Integration," *Systematics*, Vol. 1, No. 1, June 1963. Dr. Rolf's early work was influenced by M. Feldenkrais, *Body and Mature Behavior*, New York, International Universities Press, 1949.

speaking, some muscles shorten and thicken, others are invaded by connective tissue, still others become immobilized by consolidation of the tissue involved. Once this has happened the physical attitude is invariable; it is involuntary; it can no longer be changed basically by taking thought or even by mental suggestion. Such setting of a physical response also establishes an emotional pattern. Since it is not possible to establish a free flow through the physical flesh, the subjective emotional tone becomes progressively more limited and tends to remain in a restricted closely defined area. Now what the individual feels is no longer an emotion, a response to an immediate situation, henceforth he lives, moves and has his being in an attitude.

Rolf describes in detail the aberrations of the physical and emotional health which may occur as a result of body imbalance:

The man whose predominant set is fear will certainly betray it in the carriage of his head, neck, shoulders and rib cage. His defensive lack of ease will show as physical as well as psychological tension. There may be physiological imbalances of many sorts, e.g., a disturbance of the sympathetic-parasympathetic nervous balance which must be present for the maintenance of good digestion: tensions and irregularities of the rib cage itself may become apparent as asthma, even as a disturbance of normal cardiac function. A head consistently thrust forward gives rise to an anterior displacement of the neck which will not be accessible to voluntary correction, nor to the directive: "Get your head up!" The resulting symptoms may vary from repetitive headaches to a shoulder bursitis. Various visceral functions too, can be affected through restriction of the vagus nerve.

Rolf proceeds to describe the ways in which not only emotional but physical trauma, childhood or sports accidents, etc., can also upset the body-balance. Such accidents lead to a series of bodily compensations, which may give rise to physical limitations and distortions and a feeling of weakness or instability in the body which is then transmitted to mental or emotional states.

But what is a "normal" body? What does it look like when it is functioning properly? Rolf has a very specific concept of the ideal end result of her work based on human evolution, a knowledge of the anatomy and physiology of the body, and her long experience with bodily manipulation. Normal body alignment is for the purpose of attaining these results: 1) movement is performed with minimum work, that is minimum expenditure of energy, 2) motion can be initiated in any direction with maximum ease and speed, 3) movement can start anywhere with minimum preliminary adjustment of the body, 4) structure is appropriate to the most adequate functional position of internal organs and nervous system, in other words, the organs are not crowded or unsupported, and, 5) there is minimum "wear and tear" on the parts of the body. If these criteria are attained, the body will last longer, be physically healthier, move more quickly and gracefully, have more energy and stamina, respond more quickly, and be capable of more appropriate feeling.

Alexander Lowen, a psychiatrist interested in integrating bodily and emotional states, lays great stress on the assertion that all neurotic problems are manifested in the structure and functioning of the body. This thesis implies that by proper training in what to observe, a great deal about a person may be discerned merely from looking at him. Lowen describes these connections very persuasively:[2]

> There is no neurotic problem which does not manifest itself in every aspect of the individual's function. . . . Because we express our personalities or character in every action and in every attitude it becomes possible to determine character traits from such diverse expressions as handwriting, the walk of the person, etc. . . . Most important, however, is the physical appearance at rest and in movement. No words are so clear as the language of body expression once one has learned to read it. . . . [Each part of the body is the repository of some difficulties.] The legs and the feet are the foundation and support of the ego structure. But they have other functions. It is through our legs and our feet that we keep contact with the one invariable reality in our lives, the earth or the ground. We speak of a people as being "earthy" to mean that they have a good sense of reality. The contrary, "to be up in the air," denotes a lack of contact with reality. . . .
>
> The lack of contact with the feet and the ground is related to another common symptom, falling anxiety. This symptom is manifested in

[2] A. Lowen, M.D. *Physical Dynamics of Character Structure,* New York, Grune & Stratton, 1958, pp. 87–94. Reprinted by permission. Lowen's major early influence came from Wilhelm Reich. See, for example, *Character Analysis,* New York, Orgone Institute Press, 1949.

dreams of falling, in fear of heights, and in the fear of falling in love. Where there is a basic insecurity in the lower half of the body, the individual compensates by holding on with arms and eyes to objective reality. One may question why I include the fear of falling in love with symptoms of basic insecurity. Of course the very expression "to fall in love" relates this phenomenon to the others, but we also know that to fall in love is a form of ego surrender. All forms of falling anxiety translate the fear of loss of ego control.

We direct our attention first to the posture of the individual. Is he straight, swayback or hunched over forward? . . . When the weight of the body is directly over the heels, the standing position can be upset easily by a slight push backwards. Here again the common expression describes the situation well. We say of such a person that they are a "pushover." When used with respect to girls it has only one meaning. I had a patient whose main complaint was that she couldn't resist the sexual aggression of men. In a standing position she tended to rock on her heels. I have heard two expressions which describe this trait. These girls are said to have "round heels" or to be "ball girls."

. . . As an important structural element in the body, a weakness in the backbone must be reflected in a serious personality disturbance. The individual with a swayback cannot have the ego strength of a person whose back is straight. On the other hand backbone rigidity while adding strength to support decreases flexibility.

[A central concept in this approach is the breathing function.] We look to see if the chest is expanded and held rigid or soft and relaxed. A blownup chest is the invariable concomitant of a blownup ego. It reminds one of the fable of the frog who attempted to blow himself up to the size of a bull. On the other hand, a soft chest, although related to more feeling, is not necessarily a sign of health. . . . [What we look for is a relaxed structure in which the respiratory movements show the unity of chest, diaphragm and abdomen in inspiration and expiration.]

The position and motility of the shoulders are as significant to the ego functions as the legs and pelvis are to the sexual functions. Several attitudes are easily discerned. Retracted shoulders represent repressed anger, a holding back of the impulse to strike; raised shoulders are related to fear; square shoulders express the manly attitude of shouldering one's responsibilities; bowed shoulders convey the sense of burden, the weight of a heavy hand.

. . . It is not uncommon to see a broad-shouldered man with narrow hips and thin, weak-looking legs. It is as if all the energy were concentrated in the upper half leaving the bottom half impotent. We find in practice that as the legs strengthen and as sexual potency increases the shoulders drop, the chest becomes smaller and the center of gravity drops appreciably. . . . The muscles of the upper half of the body have been spared the function of supporting or moving the body. They should be soft, relaxed and available for quick, sensitive movements.

The bearing of the head is in direct relation to the quality and strength of the ego. We are acquainted with the long proud neck and the short bull-like neck which represent familiar attitudes.

When we study the expression of the face as a measure of the character and of the personality we are on more familiar ground. . . . Our attention should be directed first to the eyes. . . . It must be with some reason that the eyes are regarded as the mirrors of the soul. . . .

Some eyes are bright and sparkle, some shine like stars, others are dull and many are vacant. Of course, the expression changes. We seek, therefore, the typical look. Some eyes are sad, others are angry; some are cold and hard, others are soft and appealing.

Not infrequently two conflicting expressions are shown by one face. The eyes may appear weak and withdrawn while the jaw is strong and protruding. Or it may be that the jaw is weak while the eyes are strong. If the jaw muscles are overdeveloped, there is a block in the flow of energy to the eyes. The jaw is a mobile structure which resembles the pelvis in its movements. . . . Many expressions are related to the position of the jaw. As it moves forward it first expresses determination, a further advance gives it a fighting expression while extreme protrusion, as in the case of Mussolini, clearly means defiance. . . .

Of greater significance are those unconscious expressions which are frozen into the countenance, so much so that we take them for granted as part of the personality. I recall a professor whose brow was so raised that lines of surprise and astonishment were engraved on his forehead. No one paid the slightest attention to it, least of all the professor. Yet when one raises one's brow strongly, the feelings of surprise and astonishment are so immediate and so strong as to be disturbing. Why was the professor unaware of his expression? We must conclude that when an expression becomes ingrained into the features, one loses consciousness of it. Like our old clothes, these expressions become so much a part of us that we become aware of them only by their absence. A very common expression which we take for granted is the look of disgust caused by the retraction upward of the alae of the nostrils. Have you not seen people who show a perpetual expression of pain on their face? Are these people in pain? Certainly! Depth analysis of the unconscious would reveal that these expressions portray repressed feelings—surprise, disgust or pain.

Thus Lowen seeks out the specific relations between emotional states and their physical manifestations. Once these connections are pointed out in detail they seem to make a great deal of sense, and have profound implications.

Consistent with this approach, but applied to a specific area, is the natural-childbirth movement, especially the Lamaze method.[3] This technique is based on control of pain through conditioning thoughts and feelings in the mother, so that the childbirth experience is converted from one of great pain (in which the woman is fighting her body) into one of ecstasy (in which the mother is in harmony wih her body's natural movements and thus enhancing the natural functioning). It is indeed a superb example of working with the body structure to achieve more joy.

From this general philosophy of the relation of thoughts and feelings to the body, several approaches and techniques have developed. The Rolf technique begins with physical manipulation of the body with the hands and elbows to release and re-position chronically tense, contracted muscles

---

[3] F. Lamaze, *Painless Childbirth*, London, Burke, 1958. For a popular account of the method, see Marjorie Karmel, *Thank You, Dr. Lamaze*, New York, Dolphin (Doubleday), 1965.

and the fascia covering them, thereby restoring natural length and flexibility. The method then works to establish movement in every joint of the body to effect "the permanent change of personality, physical and psychological, which is structural integration."

An associated method developed in Europe works with the connective tissue also to release muscle tension and "sticking." The physical manipulation does not penetrate as deeply, but the technique is based on similar principles.[4] The Rolf technique, however, has as its goal the "integrating" of the body—while the connective-tissue massage is designed for release of tension.

Having the body-structure aligned so that it is fully functional, however, is not sufficient for it to function. If there are psychological blocks to more adequate functioning, the available body-structures will remain dormant and perhaps gradually return to a dysfunctional state. If, for example, anxiety over sexual functioning has created chronically tense and contracted muscles around the genital area—with resulting fatty accumulation around the hips and upper legs and immobility of the pelvis joint—then structural alteration through, for instance, the Rolf method, may realign the pelvis, free the joint, relax the muscles, and lead to a reduction of fat so that the area is once again available for natural movement. Such physical release often helps to discharge the anxiety. However, if enough guilt over sex remains, moving the pelvic area will still provoke too much anxiety and it will remain

---

[4] Maria Ebner, *Connective Tissue Massage*, Edinburgh, Livingstone Ltd., 1962.

immobile even though it has the full potential for free motion. Having an automobile that will go 60 mph is of little value if the driver is afraid to drive over 30. Integration of the emotions with the physical structure is required for a more lasting change.

Lowen's therapeutic technique involves integrating physical work on the body with analytic work aimed at intellectual understanding. For example, an individual may have felt great hostility and an urge to hit his parents, but guilt and fear prevented the direct expression of this rage. Restraining the urge to hit resulted in a bunching of the shoulder and arm muscles and a tightening of the neck—a combination that can lead to forward head, round shoulders, shoulder bursitis, and even arthritis. Lowen's approach is to talk analytically about the feelings and at the same time have the person physically hit out—in a controlled setting—perhaps pounding on a couch. Lowen will ask the patient to shout an appropriate word and in any way try to feel the angry feelings as he beats on the bed. Often the feelings take over, the pent-up fury comes through, and the patient pounds until he's exhausted. This opens up important childhood material for analytic use, and leads to the relaxation of the shoulder and neck muscles with further exercise. Thus not only have the muscles been relaxed, but the original cause of the tensions will have been dealt with and presumably no longer offer a threat to the structure.

Although it has not yet been tried, some combination of the Rolf and Lowen techniques would appear to be very promising. A combination of these two approaches should leave our ideal man with a freely functioning organism and an under-

standing of himself that will allow him to be
sensitive to inappropriate body-feeling. His greater
understanding will spur him to corrective measures
when he finds himself in a difficulty.

Following are some specific techniques aimed at
working at the level of body-structure for the purpose of releasing the human potential. As mentioned earlier, these examples derive from the
author's own experience in conducting groups of
various types. These have been psychotherapy
groups with hospitalized patients or with people
who have come together to solve neurotic problems, or, most often, encounter groups.

PHYSICAL RELEASE

When: The manner in which a person holds his
body indicates his mood, his background, and his
present accessibility to human interchange. Past
experiences have resulted in habitual ways of
holding the body which facilitate or inhibit interchange and, if the experiences are of long standing, the body attitudes may be more permanent
because of chronic muscle tensions or other structural changes. Some of these physical blocks can
be dealt with directly in the here-and-now, and
others—the more deep seated—need a longer
course of treatment.

How: Several methods may be used to open a person to change by altering his body postures.

People often sit in a group with their arms and/
or legs locked up, that is, crossed and very tight.
This is frequently accompanied by head and neck
tension, and very shallow breathing. This posture
is often a manifestation of an unconscious resist-

ance against being reached by another person. The individual is setting up a defensive wall to protect himself from whatever onslaught may ensue. It is often very difficult to communicate with a person in this posture, since he is difficult to "penetrate."

A technique for dealing with this situation is to ask him to "unlock" himself, to uncross his arms and legs and take a deep breath. Very frequently even this slight change will thrust him into the group and help to open communication with him.

For many people tension becomes such a frequent state that they become unaware of the fact that they are tense. The tension, of course, also decreases their opportunity for experiencing freely and fully. A simple method which improves this situation consists in asking everyone to walk slowly in a circle, trying to feel as relaxed as possible. Then ask them to tense each muscle in the body gradually, beginning with the face and neck and proceeding through the shoulders, chest, arms, hands, stomach, pelvis, upper legs, lower legs, feet, toes. They are to increase the tension as much as possible. Finally, the tension is slowly relaxed, beginning from the toes and proceeding upward step-by-step until the head is released. The whole procedure may be repeated. This feels very good to many people; with some it lets them realize the extent of their tension and gives them a tool for releasing it.

Various childhood problems result in a tightness through the upper respiratory tract and lead to shallow breathing and "tight voice." Often this is accompanied by coughing, occasionally by asthma. Conditions of this type often are the result of a stifled desire to shout back at a parental figure. Through fear of retaliation or withdrawal of love, or from guilt, the scream never came, but the voice became characteristically quiet and taut. As a rule, this person can't remember ever having raised his voice.

One method for dealing with this situation is to get the person to scream as loud as he can; and to do it over and over again, getting louder each time. If he is able to do it, the effects can be very dramatic. He may break into a cry, he may rage, or he may feel a great release. If he cannot yell in front of people, the person may be able to yell in the shower or while driving on the highway.

To demonstrate more precisely what occurs in these techniques, two not previously mentioned—to increase breathing, and to release aggression—will be described in detail.

BACK LIFT

When: According to the somatopsychic notions of Ida Rolf, it often happens that a tense rib cage constricts breathing, prevents feelings from flowing through the body, and leads to a sense of tightness, constriction, and a lack of vitality and/or ability to move. At these times actual physical intervention is helpful.

How: These are two ways in which the muscles surrounding the rib cage and the lungs may be restored through stretching to their natural length and fullness of breathing. The body may either be stretched upward over the head, or sideways. For the upward stretch, two persons stand back-to-back with their arms stretched high over the head, hands together. The stretcher grabs the hands firmly and dips slightly to ensure that the stretchee's buttocks are next to the small of his back. The stretcher now slowly bends forward until his back is approximately parallel to the ground thus raising the stretchee off the ground. The stretchee relaxes and breathes heavily through the mouth, sucking in and blowing out. When this rhythm is established the stretcher dips toward the ground during the inhale and rises slightly during the exhale, thus facilitating the deep breathing. This is repeated until the stretchee has had enough. The stretcher then slowly straightens to an upright position. The more chronic muscle tension developed in the chest area of the stretchee, the more painful will be this exercise and probably the less he can take. This direction of stretch usually affects primarily the muscles under the shoulder and in the stomach.

The sideways stretch is accomplished by again standing back-to-back, but this time with the arms straight out to the sides with fingers intertwined. Again, the stretcher places his buttocks directly below the buttocks of the stretchee and bends forward slowly until his upper body is parallel to the ground. The stretchee relaxes and breathes strongly, sucking in and blowing out, and the stretcher, in rhythm, pulls the arms down toward the ground on the inhale and releases them upward on the exhale to facilitate the deep breathing. When the stretchee has had enough, the exercise is stopped by the stretcher rising slowly to an upright position. This exercise usually relaxes the muscles across the chest.

After these two lifts, the usual result is that

breathing is deeper, the chest cavity feels larger and lighter, and there is better color in the face and increased feeling in the body.

Cautions: If the stretchee has any history of back trouble especially with discs, or he feels any concern about the adequacy of his back to take this movement, this exercise should not be done. The stretcher should not weigh a great deal less than the stretchee although the amount of weight supportable on the back is surprisingly large. A 185-pound man supported one weighing 270 pounds without ill effects, but such a discrepancy is not recommended. Probably most average-sized women should lift only other women on their backs.

Example: Among John's major problems were guilt and fear. These feelings prevented him from trying his best. He could never allow himself to win at anything, even though his abilities were great. In every competitive situation he tried to arrange it so there were no losers. The result, of course, was that he rarely used all of his abilities and was in constant conflict in this area. This trait was dramatized when, during an encounter group, he was challenged to Push (an activity where two people clasp hands and each tries to push the other backwards; see page 188) with another group member and the push ended in a tie although it appeared quite clear to the group—including John's adversary—that John was stronger. The group became very angry with John for patronizing his opponent and not giving him the courtesy of an all-out effort. John could only apologize, cower, and ask people not to dislike him for it. He also mentioned something about being afraid of his own aggression and strength.

Several meetings later, John was talking about his strong wish to be relieved of the guilt and responsibility that weighed so heavily on him. While he spoke, he was sitting with head down, shoulders rounded, arms falling loosely between his legs—a look of actually having a tremendous burden on his back. The time seemed appropriate to take some of the load from him physically. So John was given the back lift, both upwards and sideways. His face lit up, his reaction was one of incredulity regarding how much lighter he felt and how grateful he was to his stretcher for helping to shoulder his burden.

Shortly thereafter John expressed the desire to push again with his original adversary. This time John immediately dug in and shoved his opponent clear across the room and back again, until his opponent finally surrendered. John felt exhilarated. He had used all his strength without fear of winning, and his opponent had not been destroyed. On the contrary, his opponent liked him much more and so did the whole group. In order to present a more vital account of this and subsequent examples, I have asked several of the participants to write first-hand accounts of the events as they experienced it.

Following is John's report of what happened.

John's account: When I was asked to push against Fred, I did not want to lose but I did not want him to lose either. I knew what it was to lose and I did not want this for him on my account. So I established an imaginary line exactly in the middle of the room, and I would push him this far but no farther. I was completely bewildered and crestfallen by the group's reaction to this. Even Fred, whom I had tried to help, criticized me. Ann was the most vocal. (Outside the group Fred and I had been in competition for her time and I had backed down there too.) I felt used. As though I was some kind of Roman gladiator who had been asked to put on some kind of a show for the crowd and when I had not put on a good show they turned on me. I saw them as bloodthirsty and they sickened me. But I was lonely, and I needed their good wishes.

All that evening I had a recurring fantasy in my mind's eye, that I had pushed him back and back and it had been easier and easier and more and more fun until I finally pushed him through the window at the end of the room. Then I would see him lying outside on the porch all bloody and feel terrible. . . .

That afternoon I was asked what I would exchange my burdens for. I said I would give them free but no one seemed to want them at that price. They tried to roll them off of me but somehow it was only play-acting. Then you offered to stretch me and see if I could straighten up after having carried these burdens for so long. This was important. One, you cared, and two, you touched me. Both, at the time, seemed extremely important. My first reaction afterwards was how very important it was to the group that I get something from this but this reaction was rather fleeting because I suddenly became aware that I really had got something out of it. It was a heady, light-headed experience of suddenly being about six times as tall. My head was way up in the clouds and I found myself looking way down to the others on the floor. It was ry strange experience which continued for some time.

Afterwards, I felt obligated to do something for them. They had been so disappointed when I had not fought better that I thought maybe I could relax my scruples enough to do this again, especially if I pushed Fred back toward the fireplace instead of the window. It was close to the end of our time. Someone pointed out that shoes were a slight advantage, so I took mine off. I pushed, he pushed back. After a while he went back; I pushed harder and we went back faster. It felt good to be winning and I slammed him up against the wall. There was a lamp in the way and I heard a crash. Immediately I was horrified at what I had done. In my mind's eye I saw big pieces of the shattered globe sticking out of his back, and blood all over. But the globe had not broken and there was not any blood. The shade was a little dented. He quickly thanked me, we were overtime, and the group broke up. I was not really sure whether I had pleased them or not. I had experimented with a new kind of behavior but felt confused as to whether it was really all right for me or not, or whether it really had any application at all to the outside world.

I still feel some constraint in the use of my abilities, for fear this will alienate people. It is very true at work but I am willing to risk this fear more.

There is some history which might be helpful to you in putting all this into some kind of framework. Like you, and I suppose a lot of others, I have always felt on the outside. As a kid I remember very vividly how my father never picked me up or touched me. However, sometimes if I worked very hard and sacrificed a great deal he would notice me. I guess for me the real impact of the exercise was being noticed, touched, and picked up.

What happened: The back lift seemed to free John in two ways. Physically it actually made him feel freer: he could breathe again and he had no burden on his back. Feelings began to flow through his body. Interpersonally, it gave him the reassurance that there was someone to help him with his burden. This experience later helped John to explore some of the origins of his feelings in his childhood relations, an exploration that contributed to stabilizing John's new feeling and behavior.

The conversion of the emotional feeling of needing support into the physical act of supporting is an application of the theoretical notions of Lowen and Rolf which emphasize the close connection between the physical and the emotional. Converting the feeling into a total body-experience makes it much more meaningful. This is a basic principle for many of the methods to be described.

The next activity involves the conversion of hostile feelings to a body-experience.

BEATING

When: Becoming aware of and expressing feelings of hostility and aggression are very difficult experiences in the culture in which we live. Often feelings of hostility are trained out of the infant at an early age so that after several years it is difficult for a person even to become aware of them when they do exist. The expression of hostile feelings is inhibited by custom, fear of retaliation or embarrassment, or fear of one's own impulses. If some experience can aid an individual to contact his aggressive feelings and to express them productively, it can help to clarify and dissipate these feelings.

How: There are several activities useful for expressing anger bodily. These include slashing the air, wringing a towel, and shadow-boxing. Perhaps the most effective method is pounding or beating on a couch or on pillows. Usually the more total the bodily involvement the more effective the experience—that is, a punching movement involving only the arms and back muscles is not as satisfying as a full body smash. To accomplish the latter, the individual is asked to stand next to the couch with toes pointed slightly inward and legs about a foot apart. His arms are stretched high over the head and back. The body is pulled back like a bow, the lower jaw is thrust forward, and the face is held in an angry expression. When the arms are stretched way back they will naturally start to come forward. The person then "goes with the motion" and slams his arms down on the bed, bending his legs on the way down so as to get the total body into the motion. Emitting any noise that comes naturally such as a grunt, a scream, or words, helps capture the angry feeling. He hits until he's exhausted.

In this exercise, as well as several others described below, the activity seems false and artificial to begin with, but if it is continued it usually becomes very real. It is important to continue despite the feeling of artificiality in order to experience the feelings.

One addition to this exercise is often valuable

for people who are very frightened by their own aggression. Such people frequently hold in the feelings because they fear that their fury will get out of control and lead to destruction, perhaps even homicide. Rather than allowing the anger to continue in this precarious condition at great cost to himself, it is often more useful for such a person to release it under controlled and supportive conditions, as in the group settings described, and then to work on controlling the feeling. One way of providing this experience is to let him first beat the couch till exhausted, as described. This often allows him to realize that his anger may not be quite as horrifying as he had imagined it. Then he is asked to take the same position as before, complete with the mouth and jaw expressions of anger and the upraised arms, but to hold the feeling and the action in that position and not follow through with the blow. He does this several times, each time holding the action until the feeling and impulse to strike go away. Sometimes this is very difficult and people will be impelled to hit the first few times. Persistence, however, will usually allow them to experience the voluntary control. This can have a very reassuring effect, which is often enhanced by later discussion. The person usually feels much freer to discuss his aggressive impulses after experiencing his own ability to control the impulses consciously. Subsequent talk may aid in draining off some of the long-built-up tension.

One other variant may be helpful at times. If the aggression is clearly not being discharged on the pillow, the person may be asked to select someone in the group toward whom he feels animosity.

That individual is then asked to hold the pillow in front of him while the aggressor strikes it. Sometimes more feeling is generated by the presence of an actual target.

Caution: Anyone with heart difficulties or other physical disabilities who may be harmed by this strenuous activity should avoid it. The pillows or couch should be of solid material and a soft surface so that the hands are not injured.

Example: Tom's inability to express some hostile feelings had been immobilizing him in the group. Following is his report.

Tom's account: I had been feeling "out" of the group. Others had been sharing—some on a pretty deep level. I was feeling "tied up" inside. I felt a head of steam to get into the group and to loosen up the log-jam inside.

I began to talk of my feelings about my parents and my wife, and the difficulty I have experienced in expressing feelings toward people, especially those close to me. I wanted to work into these in a role-play or psychodrama of some kind. Bill suggested a psychodrama with a gal. I picked a gal who reminded me of Helen, my wife. We talked about a situation in which I felt she had put me in a hole and then blamed me for it. People sitting around the room acted as alter egos. A lot of material came out, nothing new, but simply underlining several things I knew already. One of these was the timidity with which I advance my own feelings, demands, and wishes, with the result that the other party doesn't know where I am and has to test to find out.

After the drama, I was talking about the inability of my father to express feelings and how angry I have gotten at him. All of a sudden, I felt that I wanted to slug the mattress. I put a pillow on the bed and began slowly going through a process of rising on my tiptoes and bringing both hands down on the bed. I went slowly and made noises as I did so. The rhythm became faster, and I began to strike the pillow harder. I got more and more involved in my speaking, feeling more and more anger until I was savagely pounding the pillow, swearing at this pillow, calling my father the strongest negative names I could think of. I became very emotionally involved in this and could visualize my father's head on the pillow. I beat him again and again and when I had him beaten up very badly I experienced a great surge of warmth and longing for him. Breathing heavily, and physically spent by this time, I collapsed on the bed and hugged the pillow saying, "Pop I love you," and such things as that. I felt thoroughly emptied and very positive towards my father.

After this, I went through a psychodrama with Tom taking the part of my father and exploring his feelings for me. We embraced at the end. It felt premature, not resolved to that degree. I embraced him largely because I had wanted to embrace the man who was taking the part in the psychodrama.

After I had recovered from the bed beating, Bill asked if I wanted to do it to my mother. I said that I was too tired and felt too much warmth for her. I didn't want to hit her. He asked if I couldn't just begin with light tapping and see what happened, and I finally decided to try it. I put her "head" on the bed as before and went through the same process. I was beginning to warm up to the subject when the face of my mother changed to that of *her father* and I began to belt him hard. Finally I was banging both of them pretty lustily. It was not as intense as before, but I got pretty well involved and became physically spent again. This time no surge of positive feeling came up. When I was through, I threw the pillow aside feeling that I couldn't care less about either one of this incestuous pair. Fuck 'em both, to quote a prominent political leader.

Net result, I felt cleansed. Felt that I was much loosened up inside. Felt I had entered the group and could now function both in terms of the group and in terms of myself.

Three months later I made a trip to see my parents, and stayed with them for a couple of weeks. I noticed some changes: I seemed more able to accept the fact that I could never make my father over into the image I wanted of him. This meant accepting the fact that there are some levels on which we simply cannot talk; there are some problems which we will never be able to solve. I seemed content to meet him on whatever level we could meet and not worry about the others. We were joking more. I was teasing him more and he appeared to enjoy it.

Another thing happened. Two of my children were confused by my father's asking them to do something for him. They did not respond enthusiastically and he became irritated and said he'd do it himself. I went to him and asked him about this. He launched into a defense about his action and I stood fast against him, pointing out what I felt were untenable parts in his position and expressing convictions opposite to his. This

was new behavior for me. I had never done that
before, and in fantasizing it, had customarily re-
sorted to violence in the fantasy. In this episode
I was able to function intellectually, presenting
arguments and actually arguing with him. We
parted amicably. Whether or not he heard the
arguments I was proposing, I don't know.

We parted at the airport, I gave my father a hug
and said, "I love you, Pop." I can feel a stirring in
my tear glands as I write this.

Relations with Mother. Became more aware of
the real hang-up she has with her old man and
his values. Real need for her to push these on people, on society in general. Felt it was just too much
to get into. Felt a real crying behind her mask.
Think I can guess at a lot of it. An incident: At
breakfast one morning, first Pop lowered the boom
on Ma for something she'd done. Then Marie, my
sister, did the same thing. A little later Ma told
Bobby, my son, he should wear a nicer shirt. I
turned on her and told her I was taking care of
Bobby's shirt. She blew a small tube and said she
was sick of everyone else's jumping on her, that
she had feelings and why shouldn't she feel the
way she did. I congratulated her on expressing
her feelings. We talked the incident through and
kind of resolved it. Later I asked her how she felt,
she said a bit better but not much. I hugged
her. It felt good to have her come out like that
on a feeling level. A great weight of trying in
her.
Summary of above: I feel I can relate more realistically to my parents in terms of who they are
and who I am. I can take issue with both of them
more easily and do so without losing what I want

to say in an overwhelming sea of emotion. I can express affection better to both, especially to my father.

What happened: The non-verbal expression of his hostile feelings let a part of Tom express itself that hadn't emerged previously. Certain feelings were consciously unacceptable, such as his resentment toward his mother and her father. Prior to the beating exercise, he could only describe his relation with her as warm and without problems, which indeed it was in general, but the unrecognized hostility was having a deleterious effect on some of Tom's other relationships, especially that with his wife, and with some authority figures. The clarification of feelings afforded by the beating reduced Tom's great confusion about the situation and allowed him to confront the actual problem. It is interesting to note that although Tom was confused, on some less conscious level he had a dim awareness of where the solution to his difficulty lay, in that he definitely wanted to beat on the couch. But while this allowed him to find the way, he needed help from the group when he resisted hitting his "mother" cushion. It was necessary for the group to enter strongly at this point to help him break through his resistance. Thus the experience required Tom's own initiative plus the group's help based on what they observed in him.

It is important to emphasize the importance of going beyond the catharsis. Bringing Tom back to the difficult situation and allowing him to use his coping abilities to deal with a realistic problem is very important for bringing a solution to the situation and engendering confidence not only in his accurate perception of the problem but in his ability to deal with it successfully. Fuller realization of his potential for coping with the situation was the accomplishment of the beating exercise. His relations with his parents were improved and his feelings about himself strengthened.

These techniques are based on the principle that feelings are represented in very specific parts of the body. Paying attention to a person's body while he recounts a distressing situation often reveals where the tension is located—whether it is constricted breathing, wringing hands, grinding teeth, knitting eyebrows, jiggling leg, hand over mouth, or wherever. Focusing on the disturbed physical area, especially through a physical release as in the back lift and beating exercises, usually helps to clarify confusion surrounding the feelings and bring them into a position to be worked on more adequately. In Tom's case, release of his generally tense feeling revealed the repressed anger, its specific quality, and targets. The followup psychodrama allowed him to work with these clarified feelings toward a more realistic relation to his parents. Often, methods of physical release are best used in combination with other techniques.

When the body activities are successful, they lead to a feeling of more freedom and an increase in the concept of the self as a capable person, both essential ingredients of joy. The principle of literal translation of emotional feelings into totally body-experiences may be carried successfully into the area of personal functioning also. Methods leading to improved personal functioning continue in this direction.

3 · Personal Functioning

Successful use of the methods so far described will bring a man to the point of being able to use effectively all the bodily equipment he has. If we are interested in optimal achievement, we must turn this very efficient car, say, into a comfortable, high-powered racer. Each aspect of the physical body can be worked on and improved over its normal state. Consideration of each organ system of the body gives structure to this exploration.

The skeleto-muscular system is the one most commonly developed. Muscles can be strengthened through exercise. Training and practice can develop greater muscular coordination, as in dance and sports. Enhanced muscular stamina and improved functioning of the respiratory and circulatory systems is attainable as is done in track. Fine coordination and dexterity can be improved as in piano and violin playing, magic tricks, games such as "pick-up-sticks." Greater muscular control can be attained through some of the Oriental methods of concentration and meditation.

The special sense organs have been developed beyond their normal capacity by specialists. Wine tasters, for example, have developed their sense of taste through training, and are able to discriminate many more tastes than the average drinker. Perfume testers have done similarly for the smell sense. Piano tuners and most musicians are able to use their hearing sense to make much finer discriminations than can the average listener. The touch of the blind man, as well as his hearing is, according to legend, more acute than normal sensitivity. The sense of sight is more questionable. The Bates method[1] purports to restore normal vision in the subnormal eye but does not claim to increase the normal ability. Special training can alert one to nuances previously unseen, such as reading X-rays and microscope slides. Similarly, the sense of touch can be trained.

In contrast to the muscles where exercise increases the efficiency of functioning, there seems to be no way of improving the sensory structures. Apparently the normal eye, for example, sees as well as it ever can see. However, improvement of the senses may be accomplished through training for increasing discrimination. When it is combined with some of the more emotional and evaluative elements, training can also increase the capacity for appreciation.

Enhancing the effectiveness of the respiratory, circulatory, digestive, urogenital, endocrine, and lymphatic systems has, so far, been dealt with primarily through the Oriental techniques of meditation and concentration, as well as some forms of exercise. The popularity of meditation is growing rapidly in this country. Perhaps the most specific symbol of this growth is the attempt to establish the Zen Mountain Center in the coastal mountain

---

[1] R. MacFadyen, *See Without Glasses*, New York, Grosset & Dunlap, 1948.

range of central California near Carmel Valley and Big Sur (for information write Zen Center, 1881 Bush Street, San Francisco 9, California). This is a beautiful 160-acre site devoted primarily to meditation. The ability to breathe deeper, to digest more thoroughly, etc., is often the outcome of better muscular balance. Freeing chronically contracted muscles around blood vessels allows blood to flow more freely around the lungs, allows for deeper breathing, etc. Long-distance running can increase lung capacity, as Roger Bannister demonstrated en route to his breaking the four-minute-mile barrier. The methods of Rolf and Lowen described earlier are effective in these areas.

Several methods have been developed for increasing sensory and motor awareness and effectiveness. Charlotte Selver, of New York and California, Mary Whitehouse of Los Angeles, and Irmgard Bartenieff of New York have evolved sensory awareness and body-movement techniques originally derived from the dance. Others have evolved different techniques for enhancing awareness of bodily sensation and movement. Sensory awareness has been an interest of Bernard Gunther[2] and others who concentrate on touch, sight, sound, and the attainment of greater discrimination and appreciation. Perhaps the most direct contribution to this field comes from Fritz Perls'

---

[2] Bernard Gunther resides at the Esalen Institute in Big Sur, California. He has developed a technique called "sensory awakening" involving methods for increasing bodily awareness. He has extended this approach to a method of hour-and-a-half-long massages also aimed at awakening and pleasure.

gestalt therapy,[3] where several exercises are described.

Development of the nervous system beyond the normal neural development occupies a large part of the formal education process. Acquiring information, learning to think logically, and being creative are ways of expanding the capacities of the brain and allied structures. Information and problem-solving are usually handled in school settings. Creativity-training is another matter. It has been considered unique, although various methods have been developed over the past several years. In scientific creativity, synectics[4] methods featuring the use of metaphorical and analogical thinking have proven very effective. Techniques of training for creativity in the classroom have been explored extensively. Artistic creativity is a more complex activity, requiring the simultaneous interplay of many organ systems.

A combination and integration of the various organ systems is involved in the acquisition of skills, especially artistic, athletic, and intellectual. A violinist, for example, must achieve a complex integration of muscular, intellectual, and emotional capacities. Muscular, respiratory, intellectual, and emotional skills must be combined for a runner or swimmer. Complex abilities like typing or mountain climbing are coordinations of internal systems to meet an external situation.

Since our assumption is that the chief source of joy is the realization and use of one's resources, it

[3] F. Perls, R. Hefferline, and P. Goodman, *Gestalt Therapy,* New York, Dell, 1964.

[4] W. Gordon, *Synectics,* New York, Harper, 1961.

follows that failure to use these resources leads to a lack of joy. Setting aside for the moment differences in emotional reactions, this assumption maintains that the master of any skill enjoys his area of expertness more than if he were not a master. A good skier enjoys skiing more than he would if he couldn't ski well. Similarly for a violinist, a wine taster, a knowledgeable person, a good typist, a healthy person, a fine athlete, and so on. The more of his abilities an individual has developed and can use, the more pleasure he feels within himself. To follow Don Quixote, joy awaits when you want to be better far than you are.

The concept of creativity is the most adequate one to express the notion of joy through the optimal development of personal functioning. Creativity implies not only the full use of one's capacities, but also includes going beyond them into previously unexplored areas. The following discussion of methods is organized around the creative process.

The creative process involves the following aspects:

1) *Freeing, or Acquisition.* Before one is able to use his experience in unusual, productive, and satisfying (that is, creative) ways, he must acquire a repertoire of experiences. He must be open to experience, able to perceive and sense his environment, and be aware of his own internal feelings.

2) *Association.* After being acquired, the experiential elements within a person must be related to each other. An individual must have the ability to associate two or more experiences which can lead to a useful product when they are joined.

3) *Expression.* Once these elements are con-

nected, they must be emitted in spoken, or written, or bodily expressive form. The association remains useless unless it can be communicated adequately.

4) *Evaluation*. Many products may be generated in the course of creative activity, but the evaluation as to which of these satisfy the situation, and which are worthless, is essential. This phase distinguishes the bizarre from the creative, and the productive from the mundane.

5) *Perseverance*. After the generation of an original idea or product, detailed work is usually in order. An enduring contribution involves much underlying effort.

The above steps can be approached not only at the conscious and unconscious levels, but also through a discussion of the role of emotional blocks. The conscious attempts to enhance an individual's capacity in the *acquisition* area is institutionalized as scholarship—the quest for more knowledge to add to an individual's repertoire. Science, the method of determining the worth of a given statement, is the social institution aimed at the *evaluation* area. And conscious attempts to increase *expression* are institutionalized as the arts, where a variety of modes of communication are developed.

However, methods of enhancement of the creative process that occur on a more unconscious level have not been institutionalized. It is for this level that a variety of techniques are being developed which give promise of widening man's horizons by affording him new access to himself, and providing means for capitalizing on his latent internal abilities.

Freeing or Acquisition

Acquiring knowledge and experience means feeding input to a human system. A person must have some materials to work with in order to be creative and to become the person he can be. He must have information and experiences that have been felt and integrated into himself.

Ability to learn is a prerequisite for the acquisition of information, but there is a different requirement for acquiring experience. Increased awareness of one's environment through better developed senses greatly increases the materials with which a person can create. Sherlock Holmes, identifying a client's region of origin from the smell of his pipe tobacco; a physician, perceiving a slight shadow in an X-ray; a psychologist, observing recurrent head scratching of a patient; a musician, noting the rhythm of a train's wheels—all these observations enhance the chances for effective behavior within the respective situations.

In addition to acquiring information and developing the senses, there is another area through which experiential elements come. Awareness of feelings and emotions allows experience to be felt and integrated into the self. The person who is open to experience, and able to feel and appreciate, has more experiential elements than the constricted, denying individual who cannot allow himself to feel deeply.

Facilitation or inhibition of a person's ability to be open and sensitive to knowledge, sensation, and feeling can occur on the various levels of awareness or consciousness. On a conscious level, sensitivity is a function of life-background, including exposure to traditional teaching methods for acquiring information about and contact with life experiences. Unconsciously, a person's ability not merely to learn, but also to sense and feel, is very much connected to his emotional development. Emotional blocks to learning are many. Many childhood experiences prevent a person from being able to learn, because of anxiety, fear, conflict, or other immobilizing emotions engendered, for example, when parental competition with a child makes test-taking so full of conflict (the child may possibly excel the parents) that the student can't study or retain; unresolved emotional problems also block off or distort perceptions, and blunt the ability to sense experience accurately as, for instance, when fear of criticism makes a person hear critical words where none exist. Problems of feeling, either emotion-flattening or hyperexcitation, are usually tied to very complex emotional problems. For example, people often cannot allow themselves to feel deep affection for others because the fear of rejection is too great. Inhibitions of this kind can occur whether the individual is experiencing inanimate objects, ideas, other people, or himself. In all these cases, the individual's openness to experience is seriously curtailed, and the repertoire of elements to enter potentially into his creative behavior is sharply diminished.

The job of helping a person become more open and enriched is therefore threefold: 1) removal of emotional blocks; 2) development of an awareness of himself and his feelings; and 3) development of a sensitivity and perceptiveness about other people and the world around him. Following are some techniques for accomplishing these goals.

THE FANTASY GAME

To help clarify the psychological elements that contribute to a person's conflict, he may be asked to personify the parts of the conflict. As a demonstration of this method of increasing internal awareness, a large group was asked for volunteers to present something to the group. To help the participants understand the feelings leading to their decision to volunteer or not to volunteer, the group leader then said to the group, "I don't really want the volunteers now, but I would like you to focus on the experience you have just had, the experience of trying to decide whether or not to volunteer. Imagine two people inside your head. One of them is telling you to volunteer and the other one is telling you not to. Picture a conversation between these two, in which they try to convince each other, until finally one of them wins. After their discussions, have them meet each other, nonverbally, and see what happens. Close your eyes for about two or three minutes and imagine this encounter. I'll tell you when to open." (The reader may find the following discussion much more meaningful if he tries this himself before reading further. The same applies to several experiences to follow.)

Following an interval of silence the participants were asked to report their pictures. The group leader made sure that they reported the way their two people looked, how they sounded, how big they were, what they said, where they were, their physical position, and who won.

The individual stories often clarify the considerations that go into the conflict, the decision-making process of whether or not to volunteer. This method helps a person to know his own feelings and thoughts a little better, and thus increase his internal awareness. Differences in fantasies were very great. Some people saw a specific person in their fantasy, figures such as their father, or mother, or a teacher; some saw no people, but heard voices; some heard one voice as very loud, or saw one figure as much larger than the other, or one form sharp and clear and the other fuzzy and vague; sometimes one figure was the individual himself at the present time and the other figure was himself at an earlier age. The technique thus helps to uncover the factors that enter into a decision, in this case, a struggle that lasted for just a few seconds. It affords a greater insight into what is happening in "inner space," the feelings inside the body.

BODY POSITION

Expanding self-awareness may also be induced by focusing attention on an individual's bodily position and feelings. In a general session with many participants, the group leader asked the participants to focus on themselves as listeners. They were instructed to listen to the leader for a short period and then write or talk about their feelings about listening. The listener characteristics to observe included: the bodily position; where the eyes are focused; feelings of tension in the body; position and movement of the hands, mouth, teeth; how the stomach feels; and what is being thought about. (The reader might try this for himself by focusing on himself as a reader at this moment.) Some people found themselves very tense, and listening quite uncomfortable; others found that their relaxed posture allowed them to wander off to other thoughts; others noticed that their eyes were focused on a fellow listener or on the speaker himself and were preoccupied with an aspect of interpersonal relations; some listened intently to each word, while others thought of things the words reminded them of; and still other people thought of apparent irrelevancies. Discussion about these issues helps the participant become aware of the many things that are happening within himself regarding his feelings about listening. Most people are surprised to discover the cues available through observation of body-postures.

Awareness of body-position is also often helpful in understanding a puzzling reaction one person has to another. For example, a member of one group was perceived as belligerent for no obvious reason since his conversation was very pleasant. Observation of his body position, however, revealed a seated posture similar to that of a boxer about to spring from his corner. The group's reaction to him was largely determined by that posture, which did, in fact, later turn out to be an accurate portrayal of a deep-seated belligerent feeling.

DOUBLING

The above activities focus on increasing self-understanding and self-awareness. There are also ways for increasing the ability to understand and feel what others are experiencing, or even how the person himself felt when he was younger. One such method is called *physical doubling*. The group leader asks the participants to imitate the bodily posture of another person and experience how it feels. Often, through assuming this posture, it is much easier for one individual to understand the emotions of another. An exchange of feelings—comparing the experiences of the one focused on, and the doubler—often clarifies the feeling for each. Doubling is also done by imitating other aspects of a person, such as repeating his words and his inflections, his facial expressions and laughter, or what he is thinking. (If there is another person present, the reader may try this.)

Doubling can be used not only as a method of understanding another person, but as an aid to experiencing the self at an earlier age. This experience may help an individual to understand the feelings of younger people in certain areas or to understand himself better by reliving a part of his past. One of the best methods for accomplishing this regression is to ask an individual to write his name very, very slowly, barely moving the pen or pencil along the page. (Again, the reader may profit from trying it now before reading on.)

After this is done, the person is asked how the experience made him feel. Very frequently people report feeling as they felt when children in elementary school. One striking confirmation of this feeling is that when adult married women are given this task, a large proportion of them write their maiden name, the name they had in their youth. This technique can be used in other dimensions as well. For example, a person may yell loudly, "No, I won't," or simply imitate younger children's speech, intensity and inflection, and the feelings of earlier life periods quite often return.[5]

Doubling also has an important impact on encounter-group meetings where it is sometimes called the alter-ego technique. The method consists of having one person standing behind another, trying to put himself in the place of the other, and periodically stating how he thinks the other feels. Also, people may exchange seats to see how it feels to be the other person. In general, this technique leads to an increased ability to understand others through exchanging places, either physically or in terms of thoughts or feelings.

ALONE TIME

Another method, a slightly different approach to increasing self-awareness, is to assign each person a thirty-minute period during which he must be alone and reflect on the events he has experienced. He is to focus on himself, his feelings, and his relations to others, and to practice the techniques of fantasy, etc., described above, and those related to association, discussed below. This activity provides an opportunity for the participant to explore himself and to provide a framework and support for introspection of a serious nature. (Try it now.)

For many people this is an electrifying experience. Several report that they had never used their time alone in this way before. For many, it affords

---

[5] These methods are discussed by Silvan Tomkins in his interesting study, *Affect, Imagery, Consciousness*, New York, Springer, 1962.

an opportunity to consolidate experience. Also, it provides a way of using alone time that may well be valuable in the future for many people.

All of these methods increase internal awareness and help the individual to know about and be able to use himself more fully, as well as to increase his understanding of others. The next step is to use these internal elements in a creative way.

Association

The second phase of the creative or self-realizing process involves associating and combining experiential elements in new and different ways.[6] The combination of gin and vermouth was a happy one for martini drinkers; seeing the relation between the structure of the atom and of the solar system advanced physics many years; connecting the configuration of logs in a fire with the shape of the benzine ring led to an important discovery in chemistry. In each of these cases, the creative act involved using elements that already existed in the creator's experience, and realizing that relating them would lead to something new and desirable.

Associations can occur in terms of information, sensations, or feelings. All are very important for creative activity. The example of the atom and the solar system is an association of information—the laws governing the behavior of phenomena in one

---

[6] For an interesting discussion of the associative process see L. Kubie, *Neurotic Distortion of the Creative Process*, New York, Noonday Press (Farrar, Straus), 1961.

realm seem to be like those in the other realm. The fire logs "looked like" the benzene ring might look, an association through the senses. Many dreams and free associations in psychotherapy are related through the evocation of similar feelings. The dream symbol of a bird of prey, for example, may represent an exploiting parent because in each case the dreamer has the feeling of being about to be pounced upon and of being helpless. The more highly developed a person's ability to associate in all three modalities, the greater his possibilities for making unusual, satisfying, and valuable connections of elements that are not obviously related.

Unconscious blocks to associational ability are many. For some people there is a fear of letting one's mind go uncontrolled and saying anything that occurs, because of a feeling that there is something in the unconscious which is frightening. Such an individual, therefore, cannot allow the free play of associations, but must keep them logical and controlled. Restriction of the ability to explore relations among various experiential elements is a serious limitation to producing unusual and interesting new combinations and, therefore, limits one's ability to develop full potential.

There are many acts of omission or commission which enhance the development of the associative abilities. Since the essence of this ability is making connections between events which are not obviously related, development depends upon the opportunity to explore freely the thoughts and feelings that the person experiences and to relate them to each other. Emphasis on imaginative games lays the groundwork for more specific training in developing the skill of associating. The following methods help a person to train himself to develop and use more productively his associative ability.

FREE ASSOCIATION

One of the cornerstones of the therapeutic method developed by Freud is the technique of reporting a free train of thought without censorship or evaluation. The assumption in free association is that the thoughts rising to the mind have a sequential connection (psychic determinism), although the person may not see their relation immediately. There is really no reason to restrict this very effective technique to the psychoanalyst's office. It is a method which can be applied with profit to problem-solving. If a person has been working on a problem, the group leader may say, "Just say anything that comes into your head, no matter how silly or foolish it may seem or how quickly it passes through your mind." By following this train of thought and having confidence in its relevance to the problem, the person can very often arrive at the solution. An example from another context illustrates this process.

Several years ago, Mr. Franklin, a business executive, was driving home thinking about football when an unusual thing happened. He was thinking about the Tulsa football team and their ace passing combination, Glenn Dobbs to. . . . He couldn't think of the name of the pass receiver, although he knew it very well. After trying for several minutes to recapture the name, he decided to see if his memory would recover if he free-associated. He immediately thought of one of his subordinates, Harry, who was about to take another job. ("Funny thing to come to mind," he said to himself.) Harry had told his friends that he had really done the work on several deals for which Mr. Franklin received credit. This had angered the executive. Association led Mr. Franklin back to his football story. He recalled that when Glenn Dobbs started playing professional football without his collegiate pass receiver, he had not done well at all. "Hmmmm, perhaps Dobbs's skill as a passer was due to his receiver rather than his own ability." And so Mr. Franklin was led to the realization that he was a little apprehensive, since if Harry really was doing all the work for which he received credit, Harry's leaving might diminish Mr. Franklin's performance, just as had happened in the case of Glenn Dobbs.

To get even, Mr. Franklin was showing Harry (symbolically, the pass receiver) that he wasn't even important enough to have his name remembered. Once he had this realization, the name of the receiver readily came to mind—Saxon Judd.

Another example occurred when a group member was exploring his possible anti-Semitism. The trainer asked him to associate to the word "Jew," in a group where there were several Jews. He did, but then someone felt that the associated words would apply to anyone. To test this, he was then asked to associate to the words "Protestant minister" and it became very clear that the associations were vastly different. Thus, attitudes were revealed very quickly to both the listeners and the associater himself, which might have taken much longer to reveal.

The reader may try this next time he forgets something, with the faith that whatever comes into his head is relevant. Free association is a valuable method that can be cultivated and used to help gain access into one's inner world.

Learning to associate remote elements can be developed by encouraging analogy.[7] The question, "What is this like?" or "What else does it remind you of?" establishes the habit of making connections within one's experience.

A variation of a parlor game is one method for developing this habit. In one encounter-group workshop, all groups were assembled for a general session. Participants were asked to express their reactions, in analogical terms, to a person well known to the whole group. They were asked such questions as, "If he were a color, what color would he be?" or "What kind of food?" or "Which country?" or "What type of literature?" or "What kind of furniture?" or "Which period in history?" or "What animal?" or "What part of the body?" or "What smell?" In each instance, the participant was to answer by expressing the essence of the subject rather than anything factual. For example, one would not give the answer "apple pie" for the food, just because a person is a United States citizen. Rather, one might think of his character, as one person did, as being bland, and express this as "mashed potatoes without salt." It is a game

---

[7] W. Gordon's *Synectics* (see footnote on page 60) has an interesting use of analogy in industrial problem-solving.

caught onto rapidly, and is very effective for stimulating analogical and associational thought.

Also encouraged was the use of direct analogy for expression of feelings. For example, to express feelings about group members in terms of family figures, or colors, or in terms of how one would like to touch them, gives a wider range for discovering and expressing true feelings.

It is often useful to bring this technique to an immediate situation. A group of businessmen were having difficulty in allowing themselves to know or think about how they responded to the group leader. Consequently, the leader asked them to express their feelings toward him since he felt there were many strong reactions and that holding back these feelings was blocking group progress. No replies. At the time the group members were seated around a table drinking water from paper cups, many of which were scattered about the table. Attempting to break the impasse, the group leader rephrased the question. He asked them to suppose that he were a paper cup—what would they do with it? Thud! Three people immediately smashed the cup in front of them. Another said he wanted to put it high up, as on a pedestal; several wanted to drink from it; one wanted to push it aside and not look at it; and one said he would "piss in it!" The externalization of the leader had allowed the feelings to come through, and the log-jam was broken. Feelings toward the leader were then discussed in detail.

Here again is an application of the principle of converting a feeling into a physical action as a vehicle for clarifying the feeling.

HUMMING

Another method, similar to free association, that also provides an avenue to the unconscious, is the use of humming. It tends to uncover the thoughts or feelings preoccupying an individual, and of which he is unaware. For some people, humming the song that spontaneously comes into their head, and then reflecting on, or associating to the words, can lead to a better understanding of the original puzzling situation. Either the title of the song, or the lines that the person has chosen to sing or hum, or the mood of the song, may contain the meaning of the association. (The reader may try it now by just starting to hum until some melody forms itself.)

This notion was once introduced at a general session like the one above, and all participants were asked to start humming. One man started humming, "I feel witty, oh so witty," to a tune from *West Side Story.* This served as an excellent example of the method because, 1) he had just made two jokes to the total group that had elicited great laughter, and, 2) because the line was misquoted. In his humming, he had reached over the first line of the song ("I feel pretty") to the second, to pick out the word that expressed his feeling. He was quite unaware of the connection between the song and his present behavior until it was pointed out.

In another example, the author was about to give a lecture to a large audience. I felt very confident and chatted amiably with the man who was going to introduce me. Things seemed under control as I hummed a little tune. Reflection on what I was humming revealed it to be the theme from the movie *The Great Impostor*. Realizing that my breezy manner didn't quite reflect my true feeling, I suddenly fell silent and reviewed the outline of my speech more conscientiously.

In another case, a patient was approaching his therapist in a particularly expansive mood. His therapy was going well and his confidence in the therapist was increasing. These feelings were brought to his awareness very sharply when he realized that all the way to the office he had been singing, "I'll make up for everything the world has done to you." Apparently he was singing his wish that the therapist was about to right all of his wrongs and give him a new start.

Humming is an enjoyable and simple method for uncovering hidden feelings that are not easily accessible to conscious thought.

Practice with these very simple methods can build confidence in the associative ability. Everyone has the capacity to associate, most to a remarkable degree. But the full use of this valuable ability requires realizing its presence, removing emotional blocks to letting it go without controls, practicing it, and gaining confidence that it works and can be a highly valuable aid to thinking, creativity, and increased internal awareness.

Expression

Internal thoughts and feelings must be expressed in some fashion. Scientific discoveries are written in technical language; music is written and played; other creative feelings are painted, sung, danced, spoken, acted. In some way a person must communicate his experience through the use or posture of his body or some part of it.

Perhaps scientific and artistic creation differ in their relative emphasis on the expressive aspect of the creative process. In scientific creativity, the primary focus is on the first three phases of the creative process—*acquisition, association,* and *expression.* The great discoveries of Freud came through his sensitivity to and integration of the material of human personality. His writing about these discoveries was only in a minor way an integral part of his creativity. It served primarily as a vehicle for communicating these ideas. A writer, poet, artist, or dancer, on the other hand, must concentrate more on the form in which his discoveries are expressed. We honor Browning, not simply for the conceptions behind his poetry, but for the very form of expression itself. When Katherine Dunham or Margot Fonteyn dance, the artistry is largely in the superb movement of their bodies, the mode through which their feelings are conveyed.

Conscious, logical factors that enhance a person's ability to express himself involve a traditional educational area, the learning of skills. Learning to dance, or sing, or paint, or write is a part of expanding one's ability to express himself. Further, the development of skill in the use of symbolism, of expressing feelings derived from one medium in terms of another, is very central. A good example of this occurs in Walt Disney's *Fantasia,* in which musical compositions are represented in visual form.

Unconscious factors that inhibit the expressive

ability often derive from cultural or interpersonal censure. The belief that ballet dancing is not masculine, or that singing in public is uncouth, or that artists are irresponsible, or that actresses are immoral, are all factors that may operate both consciously and unconsciously to inhibit the full expression of feelings in these areas. Also the unwillingness to display oneself in front of others, as in public singing, is a major deterrent to free expression. To the degree that these inhibitions exist, self-realization is curtailed.

When an atmosphere of mutual exploration of creative expression can be established, wherein the whole group is attempting to support the creative efforts of each, remarkable progress can be made.

WORDLESS MEETING

For the first meeting of one encounter group, the members were instructed that they could not use words, either written or spoken. In addition, the chairs were not arranged in the usual orderly, circular way. No group had a table. In other words, the group members simply filed into a room where the chairs were pushed to one side, and they had to relate to each other for an hour without words. This was an attempt to encourage the use of communication other than verbal. (One group followed this with a closed-eyes session in order to have the heightened experience of senses other than sight.)

This was a unique experience. The group danced, gestured, played footsie, acted out meanings, and did many other things. One surprising discovery became apparent. It seemed that a much clearer picture emerged of each of the group members after the wordless first meeting than ordinarily exists after a more traditional first meeting. Perhaps this discovery underscores the use people make of words to prevent others from knowing them.

This method encourages the conversion of feelings into actions. The group's desire to "include" a member in the group was expressed when several members literally picked him up with his chair and carried him into the group circle.

DYADS

Expression sometimes comes easier, or at least differently, when there is just one other person present. To experience this, group members may be paired, forming a dyad or two-person group. These dyad meetings last from thirty to sixty minutes. The charge to each member of the dyad is to try to understand the other, learn how to give to and take from the partner, and how to produce creatively with him. The objective is to provide an opportunity for each participant to learn to express himself and receive the expressions of another in such a way that a relationship can be built. The time allowed for this activity provides the opportunity to work through difficulties and to build positively.

The situation is unique in that participants, according to the rules of the game, must maintain the relationship and not follow their usual pattern of withdrawing from a difficult situation. This will be commented on further below, under the heading of Perseverance.

These techniques introduce people to modes of expression of a wider variety than most of us are used to, both in terms of using more sense and body parts in more complex ways, and in terms of using different social groupings—alone, dyad, small group, large group. Expressing oneself in a supportive atmosphere allows a person to experience himself doing something of which he felt incapable. Frequently, expressing the unexpressible provides such a boost in self-confidence that an individual may permanently increase his repertoire of modes of expression.

Evaluation

After experiential elements have been acquired and associated, in order that behavior be creative and useful rather than merely bizarre, it must be evaluated as to its relevance for satisfying the situation. Introducing the sound of a screeching chalk into a symphony, or ketchup into a fine liqueur, or using a paper clip to dig a tunnel— all these are unusual connections between diverse elements, but their value is somewhat dubious.

Evaluating scientific products is often less ambiguous than judging the worth of artistic ones. Usually the techniques of experimentation and testing developed by science are adequate to evaluate the merit of a new achievement. Artistic excellence, however, seems more ephemeral, and depends on the artist's own feeling of satisfaction, or on public reaction and social trends. The waxing and waning in popularity of Kafka, Sinatra, Telemann, Van Gogh, or Tiffany lampshades illustrates the difficulty of evaluating artistic achievement.

Conscious methods of evaluation have been worked at extensively, especially in the scientific realm. The whole superstructure of experimental and statistical design of experiments is an attempt to evaluate ideas or hypotheses.

Other less objective methods from the unconscious realm are also used to evaluate a product. Scientists and artists will often talk of having a good or bad "feeling" about their work. Some mathematicians have reported waking up "knowing" they had solved a difficult problem. After this insight, it may have taken days to actually work out the details, but the scientist "knew" that within him were the elements sufficient to solve his problem.

On the other hand, there is a "feel" of non-solution. An engineer reported a childhood incident in which he was building a model airplane. It had all parts but a motor. But, he reports, he "knew" that even with a motor it wouldn't fly. As he analyzed it, his "feel" arose from a recognition that there just weren't enough parts, and because he didn't know enough about airplanes to make it fly.

Apparently, in these cases, the unconscious has "advance information" about the adequacy of solutions, and signals this intelligence through bodily sensation. Ability to respond to these sensations can be very profitable in abandoning some trails and pursuing others. There will be errors, but learning to respond to the bodily sensations increases the likelihood of arriving at a satisfactory conclusion.

Emotional blocks to adequate evaluation occur

in the matter of decision-making. On the one hand, fear of disappointing others or the self, general insecurity about personal competence, or a compulsive perfectionism can prevent a deservedly favorable evaluation of a man's own productions. On the other hand, the need for wish-fulfillment, the drive for achievement, or a competitive urge can give rise to unwarranted acceptance of one's work. Conflict, vacillation, or premature decisions may result. (There are also, of course, many other causes of problems of appraisal.) To the degree that these factors are present, an individual will have difficulty in evaluating realistically his own productions and will tend either to accept them uncritically, or to reject worthwhile achievement. In either case, creative behavior will suffer.

The following technique uses these ideas regarding evaluation.

BODILY FEEL

The primary implication for training methods of this analysis of the creative process's evaluation phase concerns the bodily feeling of "right" or "wrong." People can be taught to trust these intuitions, so that if they are uncertain about a course of action, they will rely upon their feeling about it. Not that these feelings are invariably right. But teaching an awareness of their existence will allow them to be noticed and evaluated by each person. One individual may find that his "feels" turn out to be valuable all the time, another may find them useful only in certain areas, while a third may learn to use some other cues in conjunction with them.

The "feels" are sometimes called "prelogical thinking." This means that the total body is involved in resolving a problem, and there are some stirrings going on prior to the brain comprehending the problem and arriving at a logical solution. If a person can become aware of these preliminary stirrings and make use of them, he can acquire a quicker and sounder way to reach conclusions. This phenomenon often occurs during the making of important decisions throughout life. Often one has the experience that one course of action doesn't "feel right" although the reasons are not clear. Sometimes this is called "hunch" or "intuition."

Ability to use this process is often reported by creative people. Sculptors often speak of their products in these terms. They may look at a piece of sculpture and feel that it "works" or it doesn't. Most are reluctant or incapable of saying why it works or not, but they are certain of the feeling. They then proceed to change it until it does work.

Cultivation of the sensitivity to prelogical cues expands a person's capacity for making sensible judgments. It is simply a matter of training oneself to be sensitive to signals already present within, and being able to use them for one's own benefit.

Perseverance

For any reasonably talented person, creative ideas and behavior come not infrequently. However, for a truly creative contribution, an attitude of perseverance must exist. The implications of the creative idea or of the resulting product must be explored, the embryonic idea must be matured, the subject matter must be "lived with" so that it can be thoroughly worked through. There is sometimes a feeling that the product should stand as it was spontaneously produced. For most products, this does not hold. Stories must often be rewritten many times before they convey the feeling intended by the author, pictures must be worked over, ideas must be considered and reconsidered from several different approaches before the result is sound.

One issue involved in perseverance may be called the conflict between the "blind lover" and the "Don Juan." On the one hand, it is possible to stick with an idea or creation too long, beyond the point when it is fruitful. The high status accorded the term "flexibility" indicates the value our culture places on giving up an idea of one's own and being open to the ideas of others. On the other hand, an idea can be rejected prematurely, before it has had a chance to develop. The history of science is replete with cases where great discoveries were made because the discoverer persisted with his idea in the face of determined opposition. Freud, Galileo, and Pasteur are obvious examples. The problem then is to avoid dramatizing the blind lover by staying with one effort far beyond the point where clearly it will not develop into anything of value.

There are likewise many reasons for Don Juan behavior. Sometimes there is the fear of failing when the product is finally tested. Or interest may fall because the excitement of discovery is past and the development seems unrewarding drudgery. Sometimes the creator doesn't know how to proceed, since the phase of perseverance takes a different type of activity than the act of creation. Perhaps one of the most critical forces influencing premature surrender is social or interpersonal pressure. His world often tells a creator that he who sticks to his own idea is selfish, self-centered, rigid, inflexible, and pretentious.

Sometimes the inability to follow through is related to attitudes toward authority. To produce something new has, for some people, the meaning, "I can do something better than established experts [authorities]." Because they have not resolved their authority feelings, this implication is much too threatening for these people and prohibits them from carrying their idea to fruition. If the connotations of selfishness and disrespect regarding a creative act can be removed, it is very likely that perseverance can be enhanced.

There are also many reasons why people perseverate on an idea beyond its usefulness. The authority issue may enter here, too, but in a way opposite from the above. For some children or adults who are rebelling against authority, a noncreative or conforming act has the symbolic meaning of submitting to authority, a feeling they can't countenance. Therefore, everything they do must be done their way. This attitude sometimes leads to creative acts, and indeed gives strong motivation to complete the act. The difficulty is that the rebel cannot make good use of already established ideas or products even when it is appropriate. Thus, his own creation suffers.

Another factor entering into "blind lovership" is

a strong need to succeed. Sometimes a person needs to achieve so desperately that he cannot acknowledge to himself that his creation is inadequate. He feels that it can't be, it must be good, he must succeed! This may manifest itself also in what appears to be slow work on his part, but what is, in fact, an inability to let go of one part of the work and go on to the next.

The next method seems to provide a setting for developing the ability to persevere.

THE NO EXIT DYAD

At a workshop that lasts for one or two weeks, people are placed in dyads early in the week and asked to meet together for about an hour each day, often divided into two half-hour periods. The essential condition is that they continue to meet no matter how difficult their relation becomes.

This requirement puts them into a situation that rarely occurs in everyday life, where a common reaction to strife is withdrawal. Remaining together forces new modes of dealing with the situation, modes which normally have been used only rarely. This allows for an expansion of typical behavior, and forces perseverance in an interpersonal relation.

The results of this exercise are usually very good and quite surprising. The surprise is that people are successfully able to work out relationships that they felt at one point were virtually hopeless and very unpleasant. Having this successful experience enhances the potentiality for coping and increases confidence in one's ability to follow through a situation to a successful outcome. This new per-

ception of one's ability to persevere usually gen-
eralizes to other situations.

The following awareness, though not exactly a
technique, is an application of these ideas about
perseverance.

IT'S BEEN DONE BEFORE

Sam was caught up in a discussion about marriage and creativity. Some of the conversation suggested an idea to him. Why not have a premarital
group like the present encounter group, one where
some friends and relatives of the prospective
couple are invited? They are encouraged to speak
openly and honestly of their impressions about
marriage, the problems they would anticipate for
the couple, their strengths, etc. Excitedly he began expanding his idea when Violet interrupted,
"The Italians have been doing this informally for
years." Sam kept going, but soon began to feel
dampened. Violet's comment had deflated him.
She had said in effect, "Your ideas are not so new,
what are you getting so excited about?" By concentrating on the aspect of Sam's ideas which may
have been old, rather than looking at the innova-
tive part, Violet had throttled Sam's creativity.

This does not mean that the observers' responses
to creative activity should be only supportive. In
all reactions, it is of the utmost importance to be
realistic. The important consideration is to appreciate the novel parts of the product and be very
certain before commenting on the lack of novelty.
Often the idea is psychologically or personally
creative, even though historically it has prece-
dents. Further, it usually happens that the prece-

dent is not *exactly* the new idea. In the example above, it turned out in subsequent discussion that the Italians *didn't* do precisely what Sam was advocating, and the differences were very important. This ploy is used very often in business discussions with the phrase, "we tried that years ago."

The improvement in skill in the area of *perseverance*, like that in *evaluation*, results from awareness, overcoming emotional blocks, and practice. Gratification attending the ability to follow through a task to completion is very great. Many people suffer from vacillation and the difficulty referred to in the theatrical world as "third act trouble." In common with techniques used to enhance the other aspects of the creative process, perseverance methods attempt to unleash forces that are already present and, through training, develop these forces and bring them under the conscious control of the individual himself. The surge of pride and feeling of accomplishment and competence that results is indeed a major source of joy.

This completes the organized presentation of techniques for enhancing the elements of creative functioning by developing each aspect of the creative process. Two other techniques for removing emotional blocks, and for gaining more access to a person's internal feelings, have proven so effective that they will now be treated separately and in somewhat more detail. One of these methods is derived from psychodrama and the other is a relatively new and ingenious method using the capacity for fantasy and imagination.

Dramatic and Fantasy Methods

The psychodramatic technique also uses the body, in that the person acts out a situation rather than just verbalizing it. The fantasy methods require an expansion of our explanation of the effectiveness of the methods, since they do not involve physical movement, but rather the full use of the imagination. The methods will be described first and then the explanation discussed.

The techniques of psychodrama developed by Moreno[8] and his co-workers over the past several decades offer a rich variety of methods appropriate for incorporation into the present approach. Just one will be described here. It is one of the most potent, and easily adaptable to the encounter-group setting. The following description will give the flavor of the method.

LOST PERSON

When: Frequently, the loss of a significant person early in life has a traumatic effect upon the child.

---

[8] The pioneer work of J. L. Moreno in the areas of psychodrama and sociodrama has introduced several approaches compatible with or occasionally identical with some of those presented here. His emphasis is on doing—that is, acting out—rather than merely talking about the phenomena in question. The Moreno Institute conducts nightly demonstrations of the technique at 236 West 78th Street in Manhattan. Also see J. L. Moreno, *Who Shall Survive? A new approach to the problems of human interrelations,* New York, Nervous and Mental Disease Publishing Co., 1934.

Later, this can have serious consequences for his adult relations with others. Whenever this situation is suspected and seems to be interfering seriously with the present functioning of the individual, this technique may prove very helpful.

How: The procedure involves two methods used in psychodrama, *alter ego* and *role reversal.* The central person, or protagonist, is asked to select someone in the group whom he feels is similar to the lost person and role-play with him the situation of meeting this lost individual. If the latter is dead, the protagonist imagines himself going to heaven for the meeting. The scene begins with a conversation about how the protagonist tells the lost one his feelings about him. After a few interchanges, the protagonist is asked whether or not the role player is portraying the lost individual accurately. If he is not quite right, the roles are reversed and the protagonist plays the role of the missing one. This technique of *role reversal* is used several times as appropriate to help the protagonist feel how the other person feels. Other group members are invited to *alter ego,* that is, to stand behind one of the principals and say things they think the principal is feeling but not saying. Usually this combination of role reversal and alter ego brings out the major elements of the situation and allows the protagonist to explore and feel the full dimensions of the issue. The action is closed by having a realistic solution enacted, where the realism is now based on all the revealed issues.

Usually the group leader or an experienced member is the director, although when the group becomes experienced all group members can participate in the direction of the enactment.

The protagonist may select the actors he wants to play other parts, or they may volunteer, or sometimes it may be more useful to have him play to an empty chair. He changes chairs as he plays both parts.

Caution: The technique is part of the psychodramatic method and usually is most effective when directed by someone familiar with that method. It tends to be a very emotionally involving method and in unskilled hands can leave the protagonist in some distress.

Examples: Deborah's father had divorced her mother when she was twelve, and had left home. Deborah knew that he had remarried since then and had more children. When she was about fourteen he had asked her to spend the summer with him, but for some circumstantial reasons she didn't go. Now, at forty, Deborah had never seen her father since, although she admitted to always being vaguely in search of him. Currently she was having a great deal of difficulty with her husband, particularly in the area of feeling much and giving much to him. As the discussion proceeded, it became clear that she may have not been able to give herself fully to her husband because she had never resolved her feelings for her father. It seemed then that the best way to deal with the marital problem was to start with the father relationship.

Deborah was asked to select someone most like her father from the group. One man came to her mind immediately. Then she was asked to enact with him the hypothetical scene in which she finally meets her father. The other members of the group were invited to double whenever they wished, that is, whenever they thought that Deborah or her "father" were not saying all they felt. Deborah began by asking the father his name, and then identifying herself by her maiden name. Just as she began to say her name she began to cry. This continued for ten or fifteen minutes with Deborah crying and her "father" holding her. The group, of course, was very surprised, moved, and teary. It was especially surprising since Deborah had been quite closed and uninvolved in the group prior to this. Finally, after the group had sat silently while Deborah cried, she stopped. At this point it was very important to continue, although Deborah was very tired. What had occurred was catharsis, but it just opened the door for further work on the problem and was not an end in itself.

She continued the meeting scene, telling the father how she felt. She seemed to be omitting her hostile feelings, so one group member played her alter ego and Deborah could begin expressing them more easily. It became apparent that Deborah hadn't thought much about her father's situation, so she was asked to reverse roles and play her father. This enabled her to better understand how he might feel. At one point her mother was introduced into the situation in the person of another group member, and Deborah played, at various times, all three roles: self, father, and mother, to get a sense of what was happening in the trio. Finally, it seemed that Deborah was really becoming exhausted, so she was asked to talk to her father and try to work out a realistic future with him now that the many aspects of the problem had been somewhat experienced and understood. This was accomplished nicely and they ended in a fond embrace, with a more rational understanding of the situation.

Several other things could have been done with Deborah; she could have confronted her father's second wife, or his other children, or gone back and talked to her husband. But it seemed that what she did was the most immediately important and drained all the energy she had. It was unlikely that she would have been receptive to any more exercises at that time. After this her mood changed radically and she became much happier and more effusive, a feeling that lasted during the remaining days of the workshop. Following is her own report of the episode and the events and feelings surrounding it.

Deborah's account: When I really got plugged in emotionally at that group was when everyone walked off and left Alfie *alone* in that room. [The group had left alone a group member who felt rejected, so that he could experience the feeling of being abandoned. Deborah couldn't do it, and returned to be with him.] Inside me was the recurrent feeling that *if* he needs someone then someone will be there. Not that someone would or could *do* anything but that he wouldn't be left completely alone.

The second thing that had impact was when one of the girls was describing her feelings about her father's closeness and concern, telling her what a precious thing she was to him (her hang-up was too much father, mine too little) and again the impact of, "I wish my father would have told *me* these things."

The next thing was your direct confrontation,

"You never talk about your husband. Why?" Because it's damn hard for me to admit failure (rejection) again—first my father, then my first husband, and now my second husband.

When you said, "Pick out someone in the group to be your father," Tom came to mind, and when we were there and he was holding on to me and I felt his arms and looked at them, they were like my father's: muscled, brown with light-colored hair, kind of springy hair. (Tom is my father's name, too.) When I sat on that cushion and looked at him, the intensity of feeling was enormous. I had no feeling of my body extremities. Just deep inside, somewhere behind my umbilicus, a gathering of something into a huge ball, soft and mushy outside and hard as steel at the core. It kept moving up past my stomach, exploding in my chest and gushing out through my head, mouth, eyes, ears, nose. The pain began with the gushing, increased with the upward movement, and became unbearable with the explosion. My chest was tight and kept trying to push it back down.

All during this time, I could only look at Tom's face, mostly eyes, and when I said "I'm Deborah Donlan," it really broke loose. I have never felt like that before nor have I ever cried like that before. Every noise, sob, cry which came out was coming from the same place that the original one came from only they were not so large or hard-cored, and they gradually diminished in size. The pain kept diminishing also in relationship to size. I had no awareness of anyone else in the room. There was only Tom and myself. In between the noise and pain the awareness of his arms around me and the hanging on to him, the feeling of being enfolded, the feeling of comfort, the feeling of "I'm home, at last," the feeling of peace, serenity, and happiness began to gain dominance and profundity.

It is incomprehensible to me, even now, that I could have had all that inside me and had no awareness of the fact that it was there. However, at that point I didn't care about the whys and wherefores, but only that it was out, and it was just great. Then I felt really loosened up and felt available to everyone else. During the subsequent time of the group, I had that beautiful feeling inside of being at peace with myself and the rest of the world.

I still can't get onto hostility/anger regarding my father, but maybe it's just not time yet. I'm sure there is quite a bit directed towards my mother. My mother and father divorced when I was nine years old with great bitterness on my mother's part, which she expressed in depth and detail as to what a rotten guy he was. However, he came to see my brother and me on occasion (which mother primed us for, to be sure and ask him for money) until I was twelve. Whenever he did come, we would go on to the airport or Cleveland and fly in the plane or a blimp. It was a marvelous, happy feeling. Those things were a blast. I never saw him after that age, however. That made me feel I wasn't worth much. He had remarried and he wrote to me infrequently. Mother told me to answer his letters and to ask for money. I hated doing this. He had gone into the Naval Reserve when I was seventeen. He sent me money for tuition and books for a year at the University. That made me feel good.

That spring both he and his wife wrote and asked me to come to California and spend their leave with them and go to Yellowstone Park. I was happy about their invitation, but my mother had hysterics and said that all he wanted was a baby-sitter, and if I went I could never come home again. I felt hate for her. At that point, I wrote that I couldn't come out to California, and I have never heard from him since. At that time, I felt like a coward, but also felt I didn't deserve any better.

Over a period of time, I had thought that was all there was to it and that it had no effect on me and my life. (How wrong can one be?) Having achieved some measure of success professionally, I began to have a recurrent fantasy and dream of meeting him. This developed in frequency and intensity when I was about thirty (about the time I had reached the conclusion that my first marriage was not working out). I had never worked through the fantasy beyond the initial confrontation. The recurrent themes were: I would find out where he was, I would go there, I would talk with him, and would tell him who I was. I always had the hopes that he would be proud of me, he would be happy to see me, and all would be joy.

I have never had a fantasy or dream since the experience in the group about my father and although I would like to see him if I could, I don't have that tension or anxiousness about it. The need doesn't seem to be there.

You are absolutely right about the draining of energy. The tension of trying to push it up and trying to suppress it, or its trying to push up and out and struggle to give up control and the struggle to not "fall apart" for years does deplete one, down to the bottom.

Also, it's such a joy to find the feeling of release that is part of the reward for the struggle, and I feel that's part of the whole need and process. Painful as it was, the peacefulness far outweighs the pain.

A second example illustrates the method applied to a death rather than a separation. It had been noted in one group that Ben was somewhat immature and seemed to lean heavily on the authority figures, idolize them, and make them omniscient. Ben was a young man in his early twenties whose father had died when he was five. He had never really experienced the grief. The account of his father's death given him by his mother had been accepted, and he never reflected on the situation again. Because of his difficult relation with authorities, it seemed promising to explore the feelings surrounding his father's death in order to understand and clarify the authority situation.

He was asked to imagine himself going to heaven, meeting his father, and talking to him about the circumstances surrounding his death and the subsequent events up to the present. He selected a group member most like his father to play that roll, and began discussing his feelings around his father's death. He frequently traded roles with his "father," his "mother" was brought in and he reversed roles with her, and several group members served as his alter ego. He discussed missing his father, what effect it had on his later life, whether or not his father would be proud of him, hostility toward his father, his father's attitude toward his mother and vice versa. Through all of these he was very involved and very depressed as the drama unfolded. Finally the accumulated emotion overwhelmed him and he buried his head in his "father's" lap and began to cry. The cry was one of the most incredible imaginable. It lasted for twenty or thirty minutes without stopping. It varied from crying without tears, to sobbing, to crying without noise, to an infant's tears, to a tantrum, to a quiet wail. After it was over, a long silence claimed the group. Slowly a discussion began of the impact of the event. One of the group members had a sudden insight that explained the crying. It sounded as though he had cried out all the crying he had never been able to get out—almost in sequence, backwards. Starting with an adult cry, he progressed backward through adolescent crying, childhood crying, and even wailed like an infant. All the crying that had been stored up and suppressed had finally been unleashed. He felt exhausted and exhilarated.

He was a very relaxed man thereafter. The dependency lessened, the voice became firmer, and the feeling prevailed that he had worked through much of the unresolved feelings for his father, and was ready to meet his peers more realistically. Ben was immediately put back into the dramatic situation and a realistic solution of the relation between a son and a dead father was elaborated upon.

What happened: In both these examples the original abandonment, happening at a very early age, had a devastating effect on the child, an effect that was quickly covered over. The covering al-

lowed the immediate sorrow to be bearable but
took a profound toll on the basic personality.
Deborah's relations with men were badly distorted,
and Ben's relations with male authorities and with
women, when it came to his being a man, were
sadly immature. The suppression Ben required in
order to endure the original abandonment acted
as a cork on all the feelings surrounding the event.
The dramatic reliving of these situations exploded
the cork and the repressed feelings flooded out. In
both cases, the relief was monumental. This release was essential to their psychological progress,
but equally important was the subsequent conclusion of the relationship, and the following up
on the catharsis to a realistic relation with the
lost person. The events were so shaking that the
full effect will not be known for several months,
perhaps years. But all indications are that these
two people have entered a new phase of emotional
development. Through the experience they were
able "to bear with unbearable sorrow" and thereby
gain renewed self-esteem and freedom from the
burden of that sorrow.

The second technique worthy of special mention
is the use of fantasy, specifically the method derived from the "guided daydream" or "initiated
symbol projection."[9] These methods, only recently

---

[9] The fascinating and powerful fantasy methods
have been developed primarily by two men. In Ger-
many, Hanscarl Leuner of the University of Gottingen
has developed the "initiated symbol projection." An
article describing the method, "The use of initiated
symbol projection in psychotherapy," is available from
the Psychosynthesis Research Foundation, Room 314,
527 Lexington Avenue, New York, N.Y. 10017. The

developed, have a profound power to deal with very deep material in a very short time. It appears to be the method of choice when the deepest unconscious material is sought. The method has great untapped potential and is so exciting and dramatic that several examples will be presented, including first-hand accounts from those experiencing the fantasy.

FANTASY—THE GUIDED DAYDREAM

When: For some people, in some situations, defenses are too high for verbal or even sometimes non-verbal methods to work effectively. If the person has some awareness of the situation, his resistance prevents anything significant from occurring. The fantasy methods are extremely effective for these situations since they allow a nonconscious part of the personality to take over.

How: The fantasy requires relaxation on the part of the participant. For this reason, lying on the floor is often helpful. Ordinarily the person is then led into the fantasy by the guide, with a specific image. Then the fantasizer shuts his eyes, attends to the images in his mind, and reports them to the guide. He must not try to force pictures that he wants to see, though after a very short time that will rarely be possible in any case. Instead he should try to observe his own imaginings. The guide enters into the fantasy at various points to

---

same group has available "The directed daydream" by Robert Desoille, who developed his method in France. Desoille, who died very recently, develops the theoretical basis of his method in some detail in his publication.

facilitate the experience. His function is to induce the fantasizer to face difficult or painful situations, or to provide help and support to meet various obstacles, or to help see the image more clearly or tie various segments together. The fantasizer frequently experiences a wide variety of emotions, including fear, elation, laughter, crying, tension, depression, relaxation. The guide allows the fantasizer to leave the fantasy when he feels that his actual feelings are positive and largely untroubled. *Caution:* This technique should not be attempted without the aid of a professional. There are many starting points for fantasies, many of which are described in the literature, and experience suggests which should be used for which situations. The type of intervention also requires experience, and the various situations that can be unproductively upsetting must be known.

Example: The Cave. Rose was very afraid of groups and only after great anguish and urging had agreed to enter the encounter-group workshop. After several days, she seemed to be feeling somewhat better and more willing to participate. Furthermore, she seemed to be able to express her fears and other emotions rather freely. For these reasons she was asked to be the subject of a fantasy to be presented in front of the total laboratory of about forty. Reluctantly, she agreed. Following is her description of the experience.

Rose's account: I was told to imagine myself in front of a cave. (*Guide:* The cave has a large door on it and there is something behind the door trying to get out. Go up to the cave, open the door and see what happens.) The door is heavily bolted and it takes every ounce of strength I have to release it. As I enter, I see two very large eyes bouncing around in the pitch dark of the cave. I am very frightened. (Can you go over to the eyes?) No, I cannot. It is very dark except for a very tiny window throwing a streak of light. Suddenly the room is well-lit. I realize I am standing in the middle of a doll house. The furniture is all very tiny. (Can you go over to the eyes now?) No. (Are they still there?) Yes. They keep bouncing around all about me. I am bewildered and somewhat embarrassed by the small furniture. (What about the eyes, can you approach them now?) No, I am very bothered by them. (Would it be easier if someone were with you?) Yes, I think it would be. (Choose whomever you want.) Suddenly I am aware of someone standing next to me, taking me by the hand, and leading me towards the eyes. It seems so natural, this person is my husband, but I am very upset over the fact that it is. He leads me to the eyes which turn out to be nothing but a large piece of paper on a wall with a drawing of two large cartoon eyes on it. My husband immediately disappears and I pull the paper from the wall, crumple it, and throw it away. I become very relaxed and somewhat angry at myself as I begin to realize what some of this fantasy is all about. (Would you like to continue in the cave?) No, I would much rather leave. It is very bright and sunny outside, and I am very relieved to be there with the smell of fresh air all about me.

This is a condensation. The fantasy actually took about twenty-five minutes. Rose had a very relaxed, contented look as she opened her eyes, in sharp contrast to the pained, tortured, tense expression that characterized her face during the early part of the fantasy.

The next day, she said she had been thinking about the fantasy for hours during the night. At first she thought the eyes represented the audience, then she thought they represented her small group, then it occurred to her that they really meant all people. She noted that she felt much more comfortable in the group and, indeed, behaved that way during the rest of the lab. Her report continues:

I thought a great deal about this fantasy and tried to piece it together. The fact that I had been so dependent upon my husband was reinforced by his having to lead me by the hand to the eyes. This dependency also was realized by the doll house, representing the little girl part of me. My fear of certain types of people came through in the eyes, as they seem to represent all people by whom I am threatened. I was truly excited over having this experience, for it opened a great many new doors for me.

One consequence of the fantasy is that it has raised my search for myself to a new level. The "little girl" living with her husband in a doll-house world was not enough. I've become more adult, more willing to try new things, to be with new people, to test myself more. I experience myself as having more guts and as being less awed and less frightened by unfamiliar people and situations. But this process has not been all joy. Having tossed out the little girl, I have lost some of the comfort and support associated with that way of life. Growing up means finding *my* way and this has been and still is a difficult process.

What happened: The importance of analysis in a fantasy is still a controversial matter. It appears that significant change can occur without insight, contrary to many widely held views in psychotherapy. Rose seemed to have her significant experience *during* the fantasy, as judged by the content, that is, symbolically overcoming a frightening object—the eyes—with the help of someone whose help was needed only for the initial support and who then became dispensable; and also as judged by the bodily changes that occurred during the fantasy, from tension and fear to relaxation and elation; and as judged by her behavior immediately after the fantasy, which was quite free and relaxed in groups and continued during the following months. The intellectual understanding of certain parts of the fantasy, which came later, may have stabilized and filled out the experience, but the primary act of change had already occurred. The technique allows the person to work on a very significant problem, perhaps even one outside of the individual's awareness, and in many cases make important strides toward resolution. Thus the technique is another one that allows an individual to use the untouched capacities within to improve himself.

The fantasy seems to act like a physical medicine that seeks out the part of the body that needs assistance. If the fantasy roams free it goes to the source of a present problem, a problem often not in the immediate awareness of the fantasizer, and works on that issue. This concept may be more than a mere analogy if we follow the theorists Rolf and Lowen who feel that all emotional problems are located in the body in some fashion, either in chronic muscle tensions, or ulcers, or shallow respiration, or diminished eyesight, or whatever. In that case, the fantasy may indeed be stimulated by that body-part and the problem it covers.

Using this conception, fantasy can be combined with body-language more directly in the manner illustrated by the following case.

Example: The Stomach. Fran had been bothered by stomach pains for years. She also had exhibited some facility for imaginative thought (most people have this ability to an astonishing degree), so a fantasy seemed an appropriate approach to the problem.

She was asked to imagine making herself very small, to enter her own stomach, and then to report what she saw. Here is the experience in her own words.

Fran's account: I have been bothered by a nervous stomach for years. My inside seems to be forever churning, seething, and feeling cramped, tight, and uncomfortable. Eating is approached with anxiety and apprehension about the after-effects, and yet with greediness because food tastes good. I have had X-rays in the hope of discovering something organically wrong but there is nothing wrong.

I was reluctant to let go and fantasize, but I did. I was asked where the discomfort was located and what it felt like. The main feeling was of a wall stretching across the entrance to the intestine. "Close your eyes and imagine the wall," I was told. I closed my eyes. I seemed to be walking along a road, a road I knew, and I felt about fourteen years old. I came to a high stone wall and I knew that at the other side was a field. (*Guide:* How can you get over it?) I can try to climb over, but the footholds are small and slippery. I feel helpless before the technical difficulty of *how* to get over the wall. I will try. Yes, I'm over, but the other side is boggy and muddy and jumping down is hazardous. There's a sense of loneliness here. (Can you go back over the wall?) Yes. (Could anyone help you to get over, this time?) I can't think of anyone . . . but there must be *someone*—yes, . . . but *which* one? . . . Ah yes, Mack! Now I feel more my own age—thirty-nine. He will give me a lift over the wall. (Are you over again?) I'm at the top of the wall. Now there is a flight of steps down into a courtyard. It's like an old English college porch—quiet, sunny, with shadows in the corner. I'll walk down the steps. I feel a little alien in this place. (Can you go into the corners?) Yes—nothing there, just cold in the shadows, warm where the sun falls. (Is there any way out?) Yes, a door, a small but heavy door set in the wall opposite *my* wall. It has a big latch. (Can you open it?) Yes, it's heavy but easy. I'm out in the street now. It's a warm, sunny day. (Is there anyone with you?) No. (Is there anyone you would like to have with you?) Yes, mentally searching for someone, Lou will walk with me up the High Street. (Can you go back into the courtyard—in and out of the door?) Yes, in and out. (Would you like to be rid of the wall?) Yes. (How?) It would take dynamite to get rid of it. I laughed. (Do you have any?) Yes . . . here we go. I blow up the wall. Most of it has gone. I'll go over and look at it. There are a few stones left. I can't get those out. (Wouldn't someone help you?) No—hope dawning—well . . . perhaps . . . the people here in the group might help me. Yes, they will! Great wonderment. I see them rolling up their sleeves and lifting out the stones. I am touched by this. It's all nice and flat now. (Would you like to plant grass where the stones have been?) There is no need to, the grass is there, has been there all the time. I feel tired.

This is as nearly the story of the fantasy as I can remember. The attendant feelings were intense. I felt very tired and relaxed at the end, and rather shy as I looked at the others in the group—all men that evening. Whatever else had happened or not happened, I felt a little chastened at my lack of trust in them, and some sense of "Now it would be different."

My attitude to food seemed the biggest change in the weeks that followed that fantasy. I began *not* to regard food as potentially harmful, and I ceased to feel so resigned to painful after-effects of eating. My stomach and intestines seemed more relaxed. I was not cured, but felt more optimistic about things changing for the better.

I am tempted to try to interpret the fantasy literally, in the light of my known confusion about my sexuality and the values I hold—to say nothing of my religious experiences or my sense of intellectual inferiority! I could also color it with all that has happened since then (during a twelve month period). But I remind myself that this was one experience within the total experience of living. As such it has value, but *because* I am grateful for it, I emphasize the limitation.

The broad strokes are obvious. The fear of taking in food, the barrier erected, the painful effects, the loneliness—this is a true description of the tension surrounding the sexual act for me and the confusion I feel about sexual freedom. It also describes the technical difficulties of intercourse, which I feel, and the fear and loneliness of the after-effects. Perhaps most of all, it is a mirror of the sense of humiliation in "letting go" so that another can help me. In another way, my fear of intellectual freedom and the barriers I erect against new thoughts, which may shake my being in control, are implicit in the fantasy. Certainly there is the flavor of my matriarchal background (Anglo-Saxon!) which nurtured the idea of men's incompetence and unfair advantages.

The fantasy, together with many other experiences, has helped to improve my physical health and my relationships with others. I am now more receptive, physically and intellectually, and yet at the same time I feel I have a more realistic view of what is over the wall . . . after all, the courtyard, though sunny and calm, had patches of cold as well as warmth. It was pleasant and natural, but not the panacea for all ills. . . .

What happened: Again in this case the change occurred during the fantasy experience, without insight. To paraphrase Fran, the wall represented, at least, a sexual problem with blocking of the sexual area, represented by the courtyard, from the rest of the body, represented by the real world. Since her upbringing had stressed the sinfulness and unacceptability of sex, she had "walled off" the sexual area and made it unconnected with the rest of herself. This feeling was also reflected in several problems with the sexual act itself. The stomach trouble then represented an attempt to stop the food from entering the forbidden sexual area. Destroying the wall in the fantasy acted to overcome the difficulty in everyday life.

The revelation that others could help her (destroy the wall) was startling and characteristic. She never asked for help in day-to-day living and it never occurred to her as "proper" or that people would really want to help her and especially to help her accept her sexuality. The freedom spread to her general experience so that she was able to relate more easily to people.

It is important to note that her digestive problem was greatly improved but not eliminated. All of the problem was not dealt with in the one fantasy. Usually it is not. Instead, the person lives for several weeks with the consequences of the fantasy, noting new behavior and feelings and acquiring insight into its meaning, and then crystallizes the next level of the problem. At that point he is ready for a new experience which may or may not be a fantasy. In this particular case it may be that since Fran worked so well with fantasy, to do another in which she entered her sexual areas would be helpful, or perhaps first some analytic work exploring her childhood relations and development of these attitudes would be of further help. In any case, the individual is taken where he is and worked with as far as he can go; then it is necessary to wait until a next step can be made.

Example: The Message. This fantasy by Nora began because of Nora's feeling of repulsion at her own body. An exploration of it in fantasy seemed

promising for revealing the source of the difficulty.
The initial image to "picture two people inside your
head, one saying, 'you are a woman,' the other saying, 'you are a man.'" This was suggested because
of Nora's difficulties with her sex identification.
The following, too, is in the participant's own
words.

Nora's account: The morning of my fantasy I can
recall as if through walking in fog. The hatred of
my being enclosed in my body was now replaced
by a terrible fear of it.

This body which enclosed me had, up until then,
been ugly and a source of shame to me—now it
had become a source of terror, something hideous.
Yet how to escape from it? I longed only to un-
zip my skin and come tumbling out.

Fritz Perls came then. [He is a psychotherapist
who was present during this group.] He held me.
I can feel his hands, very firm. I can smell him.
I can see the eyes within his eyes. The outer eyes
watery and diffused, the inner eyes clear and
strong.

I'll now come back from my journey, to say
very clinically that utter despair is a prerequisite
for successful fantasy.

I could not have remained in that room for very
long if I had to remain totally conscious; my need
to escape was so powerful.

Oh Bill—your request for this account was complete with just one sentence—my reply can be as
long as the Arabian Nights!

You asked us all to picture a man and a woman
in our minds.

My man and woman were not very clearly seen,

but they were fighting. The man was screaming, "She is mine!" and the woman was also screaming, "She is mine!" Then the woman bludgeoned the man to death. At first she felt victorious, but soon she was so sorry she had killed him because killing was not a feminine thing to do. She had behaved like a man.

I see the man lying dead. He is very tall, like Gulliver among the Lilliputians. He has black hair, very straight and flat to his head and long black sideburns. He is wearing shiny boots—high ones that come to just below his knees, and black pants and a black long-sleeved sweater with a high neck. Over the sweater is a vest of chain mail.

A flock of blue birds hovers around him. Each bird takes a little piece of his clothing in its beak and together they lift him, still dead, and carry him to the top of a mountain. They gently land him and fly away. He wakes up and looks around and walks to the mouth of a cave and goes in. The roof gets lower and lower as it slopes toward the back of the cave. It is light in the cave. He sees a pool way at the back. He wants to put his face in the water, but he can't bend down because of the stiff chain vest. He takes the vest off and his boots too. He sits in the pool. Soon he wants to leave the cave and the mountain, but there is no way to get down. The mountain is shiny and black and slippery like marble. He sees a big rock in the bottom of the pool. He tugs at it and pulls it out. Then he sits in the hole and slides down. It is like a chute which runs down through the middle of the mountain. He emerges at the foot of the mountain, and tumbles out on to a grassy hill. A small country village lies below the hill.

There is a girl. She is dressed in a long pinafore that is red with blue-and-gold embroidery around the hem. Underneath, she wears a white blouse with puffed sleeves. She wears a kerchief on her head. Golden ringlets show from the edges of her kerchief. Her skin is very white and creamy. Her body and arms are rounded and soft.

He wishes to take her to the top of the mountain. He tells her about the cave and the pool. She is reluctant to go with him. She points out that there is no way to climb that steep mountain.

(I was content to leave them there until you suggested a helicopter, Bill.)

The helicopter lands, picks them up and flies to the top of the mountain and lands them there.

The man takes her hand and gently leads her to the cave. She is very reluctant to go. He convinces her. They enter the cave. She looks around and is filled with wonder. He leads her to the pool. He sits down in it. She is timid, but finally lifts her skirts and sits in it too. She then becomes worried about leaving. In answer, he shows her the big rock. As he removes it, he tells her to be prepared to slide down the chute the moment he removes the rock. He explains that they must slide down with the water or else the inside of the chute will be dry and the rocks will scratch and bruise them.

She braces herself, he removes the rock, and down they slide through the dark chute. Out they tumble at the bottom. They are wet and disheveled, his flat straight hair has become wet and curly. They roll and play on the grassy hill like two puppies, curly and wet and rolling. Then they stand up, look down at the village, and walk hand-in-hand down toward it.

While in the fantasy I was conscious of your voice, Bill, and sometimes conscious of my body, but of very little else.

The fantasy was all in pictures—much like watching a movie; yet more, because I instantly knew the thought and feelings of the players. Somehow *I* was each of them and in some way was the mountain and the chute too.

When I "awoke" it was like returning from a dream. My depression was gone. I felt a peace and sleepiness, much like what you feel after crying for a long time. I could take deep breaths.

You then asked me to go into my body.

I entered through my mouth. Slid down my throat which was the same as the chute in the mountain. I tumbled down and landed in my vagina. I was very tiny. I stood up and parted the vulva and jumped out onto the seat of a chair on which the body had been sitting.

I was free! Yet I was uneasy. I wanted to enter another body, but they were all taken—and yet I didn't want to go back into mine. You asked me to go back again. I consented with reluctance. I then decided I'd go back, but to my brain this time. I was very elated to go into my brain. I liked my brain.

I entered through my "third eye" and found myself standing in front of a heavy wooden door bound in iron, like the old Spanish doors.

I was still very tiny and had to push with all my strength to open the door. It opened just enough for me to quickly squeeze through, and then it shut with a loud slam. Inside, I saw a spring on the door which made it close so quickly.

It was pink inside my brain and very light—

very bright light everywhere. I heard a humming sound—it was that of the machinery. I inspected the machinery. It was all working smoothly.

There were very fine wires overhead. I heard a whirring noise and saw a tiny piece of paper, folded in half, suspended by a clothespin, coming quickly gliding along a wire. I stood on tiptoe and read the note. It said, "Move your feet." Many more notes came whirring in. They all had short messages written on them. I enjoyed reading all these messages to my brain. I then noticed a book hanging from the wire. It was very thick and very old, with a worn, maroon-colored binding. I thumbed through the book. I decided it was much too long to read.

You asked me then to try to read it. I turned to the first page, but couldn't read it. It was in a foreign language. You then asked if I could get someone to help me with it. Then I saw Fritz sitting on a high stool in a corner. He was wearing his jumpsuit. It was dirty. His legs were crossed at the knee and he was holding his head up with one hand, his elbow resting on his knee.

He asked if he could help me—and then I began to cry. I came out of the fantasy then. I remembered our meeting that morning. I could only remember the beauty of him and the love. I get lost in the memory of it even now.

You then asked me if my teeth could help me to read the book. [This was because she was grinding her teeth as she lay there.] I put my ear next to my teeth. I heard vibrations. If I could understand the language of these vibrations . . . my teeth were telling me something, but I couldn't understand the language. I sat on my tongue. It moved in a rhythm—the same rhythm as the vibrations—but I couldn't understand what the rhythm meant.

I went back into my brain. I opened the big book. The first page was covered with writing, but it wasn't really letters or lines; the page was entirely covered with markings, all jumbled together, filling the entire page. I looked closer and saw that it was written in many foreign languages. There were Russian letters and Japanese strokes and Egyption hieroglyphs, all mixed together.

I felt so confused and helpless. How could I ever hope to decipher those markings? I knew that they contained a very important message; if I could understand them, I would then know the answer.

You then told me to look at the first few markings. I looked closer and looked very hard. I saw the first line. There was a hammer and a sickle, a star, an X and a triangle. None of these symbols have any meaning for me. I kept repeating hammer and sickle, hammer and sickle. What do you do with a hammer? A hammer is to pound with—a sickle? A sickle to cut with. Pound and cut, pound and cut what? Pound and cut the star! I pounded and cut the star and each of the five points of the star broke off, and then there were ten points around the star. I hammered and cut more and more, until there were many, many tiny points and the star became a seal. It looked like a notary's seal. It was gold and grew very big. It was the Great Seal. The Great Seal of Approval! I hammered and cut it. It broke up into tiny pieces. I ground it into gold dust and it blew away. The hammer and sickle and star were gone. I looked at the X. X means unknown. I hate unknowns. I changed the X and made it AX. It means Accept. Accept what? Accept the triangle, but what does the triangle mean? I stared at the triangle. It became a Haman taschen. A Haman taschen is a Jewish cookie, baked in the shape of a triangle. It is eaten during the Purim festival. The Haman taschen is named after the evil king, Haman, who decreed that all the Jews in his kingdom must die.

The message then said, Accept the Haman taschen. I laughed—how ridiculous! All this work just to be told to accept the Haman taschen! The message had no meaning for me. I needed a meaning. The Haman taschen was very big, because I was still very tiny. I walked into the center of it. It was filled with prune filling and was very sticky. I was soon covered with the prune filling. It clung to my feet and my face. I wiped it away from my eyes and my nose. It almost smothered me and I could hardly breathe. It was now covering my hands. I licked one of my fingers. It tasted good. It was sweet. I ate the filling from my hands, and then ate all the rest of the filling, until all that was left was the crusty outside part. I was very hungry. I took a bite of the crust. That tasted good too. Not like a Haman taschen at all, but like a butter cookie. It was very big, but I ate all of it. The Haman taschen was gone. Just the X was left. It still meant unknown, but then I remembered that I had changed it to AX and then to Accept. The message meant Accept! It had great meaning for me. I must accept myself, I must accept my body as part of me. I cannot have just a mind, I must have a body also.

I came out of the fantasy and I was at peace. I marvel at me—the wonder of me!

How I wish you were here in the days after I came home. I wanted you to see me then—to see and know the joy! You shared the pains of the birth—but did not witness the joy that came after.

I came home to my husband, David. I saw him and loved him. I can't imagine any returning traveler being welcomed with the warmth and understanding that I came home to.

And life is sweet—but too soon the "business of living" hides living. And David goes to work and I go to school and our boys go to school and we wear our wristwatches again and put on our shoes again.

The peace remains. The joy? The joy I fear is too gossamer a cloak. It cannot withstand the buffeting winds of our world down here.

A semi-amusing epilogue to this fantasy began upon Nora's return home. She told David that one of their marital problems is now clear to her: she feels that she is physically stronger than he is. So they wrestled and he won. She is content.

But he isn't. His own concerns about masculinity are focused by this event and he feels that he must prove himself by wrestling with Nora's group leader—me. David begins a program of weight-lifting and wrestling, and signs up for one of my workshops five months hence. On the last day of the workshop he announces that the time has come. No amount of cajoling will do, we must wrestle. The next day he looks exhilarated, he has met the test. And indeed it appears that the contest was very valuable for him.

I certainly hope so. As I sit here writing, two weeks later, my ribs still ache.

I asked Nora what the impact of the fantasy is now, six months later. This is her reply.

Nora's reply: That message *was* a good one, because I had to accept all of me. Yet in the months since it also became a barrier for me, because I could not accept my body. I wanted to change it, and that meant that I didn't accept it as it was.

Two weeks ago, two friends and David decided to put me into the middle of the circle and have me break out (just like we did with Nancy). [See Breaking Out, page 190.] My reaction to being surrounded was grotesque. I was totally petrified. I finally broke away from David and one other woman. But the other man caught me and held me around the waist, and I couldn't break away. The fear of having him so close, holding and feeling me was enormous. Later that night I realized that it was the fear of his touching and feeling my body that had petrified me. I didn't want him to feel the fat and ugliness of me. And when he did, I could no longer hide—he knew my secret. Then I knew that I had been using my fat to hide behind. All my life I felt that I couldn't really compete with other women, because of my body. So instead, I became a "helper"—thus I was not a threat to them and they liked and accepted me. It worked the same with men. I could never be thought of as a woman, to be desired physically, so I became a mother to the men. The helper role was genuine sometimes, but too often it was just a role, so that they would accept me, but on "safe" ground, always intellectual, never physical. The helper role had become so integrated into my personality, that I couldn't distinguish any longer between really wanting to help or using it as a hiding device.

I don't have to be a helper anymore. I want to compete with other women and be desired by men. I don't need the fat anymore. I am getting rid of it. I will make my body beautiful.

I have no more secrets! I got rid of that last bit of debris that was clogging the stream, and now I'm running swift and clean!

The beautiful residual effects of our group never dry up. Like golden drops of honey they filter through the hive of my mind, adding sweetness again and again.

"Nora" is a lousy pseudonym for me, I don't look or feel like a Nora anymore. Nora sounds like somebody's mother—so how about Bathsheba?

The joy isn't a "gossamer cloak." It isn't anything to wear. The joy is this wonderful, throbbing core of me.

Hope your ribs are all healed. . . .

My job as guide to Nora's (or Bathsheba's) fantasy was to keep her focused on the message until she could decipher it. It was as if she had the answer to her problem within herself, but she needed outside support to dare to read what it said. Once she could decipher the message, the release followed.

The next example, including the title (after the story by Carson McCullers), is given in the words of the girl who had the fantasy. She was having affectional problems at the time—affairs of the heart—being in the throes of deciding on a divorce. To start the fantasy, she was asked to make herself small and to enter her body wherever she wished.

The Heart Is a Lonely Hunter. When the specific body fantasy was first described, I thought of the short story, and of the movie to be released soon, *Fantastic Voyage.* Inner space can be as intriguing and challenging as outer space. Since it was mentioned that you went to the part of the body that you had the most conflict about, I figured that I would probably end up down in my vagina or other such female organs as that is where I thought that I have the most trouble. Fantasies about such things wouldn't be something that I would want to reveal to members of my group, no matter how accepting they were. But when I listened to Nora with her excursion through her body I was swept along with her excitement, imagination, intrigue, and tremendous feelings. I was most affected by her agony when she "couldn't read her book." The feeling of estrangement from myself came over me and the façade of being capable, confident, self-knowledgeable, and mature was swept away.

Utter loneliness came over me with such an intensity that I cried out I was sorry that I had ever come to the workshop; that I wished I were dead; that I couldn't stand it. Rob, wonderful St. Bernard Rob, held me and rocked me and comforted me. I observed myself in the midst of this experience, and when Madeline made her insipid comment which I felt was interfering with my feelings, I yelled at her and felt good about shutting her up.

But my intense feelings were suddenly dissolved. I was willing to put off further exploration until after lunch—always considerate of others. However, Bill suggested, and the rest of the group agreed, that it would be better if I went ahead right now up in the cabin. I can remember bragging that I could produce "instant fantasy." Rob walked over to the cabin with his arm around me, and I kept crying and asking, "Why do they care about me? It can't be just because I'm a human being, can it?"

As I lay down on the mat, I heard someone say that it wasn't going to be pretty or that it would be rough or something like that. My reaction was to minimize the threat—I thought that they were exaggerating. True to my competitive spirit, I wondered if I would do as well as Nora. Would I be as imaginative and as delightful? Would my group be bored? Throughout the fantasy I was aware at times of the others—when they would laugh at the funny things or when I cried out and someone took my hand or stroked my forehead. Even as I was interpreting some of what I was experiencing, I wondered if others were as tuned in. This is what I remember happening:

Following the directions, I closed my eyes and made myself very small. It seemed artificial at first, and then I became the miniature person. I tried to enter my body by way of my vagina (as I had feared) but found it was blocked. So I went back out and climbed up the exterior of my body. I can't remember how I got in next except that I went down either the esophagus or the trachea. (I was aware of dim memories from anatomy and a certain concern for getting the names and proper location right—commented on later by a group member as an indication of my being a nurse.) It must have been the trachea—I saw round rings of cartilage and I kept going down into the alveoli. This too was blocked. The little rounded air chambers kept me from going any further.

Suddenly, I saw my heart. It was floating in my chest cavity with no attachments—just suspended in nothingness. I was very frightened by the detachment and struck by a sense of awe, in the bad way.

"Can you get across to it?" Bill asked.

"No! It's too smooth and slippery." My heart—a cross between a conventional valentine and what I know a heart to be anatomically—was very smooth, reddish, and rounded. Wet. I knew that if I jumped across to it, I would fall off—down, down, down.

(Can you build a bridge?)

I felt comforted by the idea. "I can try. I'll put a plank across." The plank was a piece of muscle, rather grey, like the whale steak that I ate in Boston shortly after I got engaged. At the time I also thought it might be like a penis, but didn't want to say this to the listening group. I put the plank across and started gingerly across. Suddenly, the plank began to buckle up and down. "It's an earthquake!" I was terrified up on my precarious perch, feeling that I would fall off at any moment.

("Can you get some help?")

"Yes. I'll call out the Earthquake Rescue Squad." This was a group of little men, like Lilliputians, who lived in my big toe. They were rather like Snap, Crackle, and Pop in the Rice Krispie ads and

wore great big Texaco Fire Chief hats. When I
called them out, they responded in great numbers
swarming all over my legs and lower abdomen
inside, running around furiously with their little
ladders. Bunglers! They were so ineffectual—
rushing around frantically doing nothing while I
kept calling to them, "Hey! I'm up here." They
didn't pay any attention to me and the earthquake
subsided. These little men were very funny even
though I was angry at them for not helping me out.
I laughed and laughed yet this easily turned into
crying. I was aware of a hysterical element.

Bill suggested that I make the bridge to my heart
more secure, so I threw a braid (human hair type)
across. At first it couldn't catch hold and finally
did latch onto a little knot.

(Can you make the bridge more secure?)

The Golden Gate Bridge came as a link to my
heart but, as so often, both of the ends were
shrouded in fog, and the two ends where it could
be attached were obscured. Suddenly it turned
into the Brooklyn Bridge. There I was, the little
darling skipping across the bridge waiting to have
a ribbon-cutting ceremony or something. There
were crowds of millions on the other shore, cheering me on. At first I was very pleased, and then
was horrified to realize that the cheering crowd
was so teeny-tiny that they amounted to almost
nothing.

(Can you get someone to help you?)

Suddenly, the Jolly Green Giant appeared and
lifted me up in his hand. He took huge steps
(three, I think) across the country and brought
me back to the West Coast. I was very grateful to
him. Furthermore, he offered, "How would you

like a can of peas for a heart?" I giggled a little at first and then became very sad. "No, thanks," I told him, "I want a human heart."

Where was it that I saw an anatomical chart of a heart with the different parts labeled? I took a pair of scissors and cut it out.

Did I go over and sit on my heart then? If so, it was similar to a picture I had taken while mountain climbing in the Tetons—me sitting holding onto one leg on a big boulder. As I sat there, the roof began closing down on me, suffocating me and crushing me. It (the roof) was like the poppy petal mask of The Laughing Man, a short story by Salinger. When I cried out, Bill asked me if I could give myself more room to breathe, and so I did.

Next I grabbed hold of a blood vessel and began a wild, free swinging in and out of my body à la Tarzan. It was exhilarating, but I finally let go and dropped into my squishy intestines. I think that Bill suggested that I get back to my heart, and so I went climbing up my vertebrae. What a delight! "Did you know," I informed my group, "how handy all these little bones are for climbing? Very ingenious!" The bones were white and very easy to climb up, rather like a ladder.

But my pleasure was cut short as I saw my heart fading away into the distance behind some hills. When I cried out in terror, Bill asked, "Can you catch it?"

I think I grew wings of some sort—a bat or a voodoo doll—and pursued my heart. When I found it, it was in a bird's nest, all shriveled up very small. It terrified me and I cried out again. It was like a little chicken liver.

(Can you feed it something and make it grow?)

"Yes, I can." All the time feeling like a tear-streaked, grubby little girl. I fed my heart (with a little beak) some Jello and birdseed with a little silver spoon. Suddenly, my heart expanded and filled every part of my body outline. Like silly putty. I laughed but was aghast at its immensity. I then regulated the feeding so it just grew a little. My heart became a little yellow canary which sang and was happy. Somewhere a yellow-and-black bee buzzed around and then stung me.

Where was it that I became frightened and lonely again and Bill asked, "Can you find someone to help you?" An Indian appeared with a large blanket. He wrapped it around me and with his arm around my shoulder, took me to his tepee. He said that they would adopt me into their tribe and I would be Little Princess Running Feet. I felt good about this. I wore a white deerskin dress with fringe. I was warned that I couldn't go over the Line which was roughly at my waist. I cried out that I *had* gone over the line; I had trespassed. (I was aware that this was similar to a recurrent nightmare I had had when I was about age five.) Also, smoke signals were sent out—S.O.S., which meant Save Our Sally.

Back to my heart again. Bill asked me something about whether I could find something nice or good about it. I saw my heart with a glacier through the middle, but the snow was pleasant, bright, and warm. I began to make snow angels in it, which was a direct opposite to the black voodoo doll earlier in the fantasy.

(Do you want someone with you?)

"Yes." A man I couldn't recognize came to play

with me in the beautiful snow. We threw snow-balls at each other, and then went into a bright, cozy, translucent igloo. My dog, Saluki, came in with us, and we were very happy.

When I opened my eyes from the fantasy, it seemed incredible that I had had this experience. There was very little comment from the others and I felt a little embarrassed that I had been so exposed. The group did give me approval for my experience and I felt closer to them because of it. I was relieved and amazed, I had no idea that I had that capacity within me. I was very shaky. For the next couple of days I didn't dare to think of any of my fantasy except maybe the Earthquake Rescue Squad for a good laugh. I erected two signposts in my mind—"Out of Bounds" and "No Trespassing"—and flashed the warnings to myself whenever I even started to think of the word "heart." When we went to the canyon for meditation the next day, I was anxiety-ridden when we had to cross a plank over a stream. It was like the plank to my heart. Also, I was initially afraid to fantasize because I didn't want to re-experience the frightening part of my fantasy. However, I was able to do this with enjoyment and only became anxious when the earthquake took over momentarily.

I see my fantasy as similar to what I have read about LSD trips, and as utterly amazing. I knew I could terminate the fantasy by opening my eyes and got a lot of comfort from my group, especially the leader. I value the experience and remember it in the detail given above, even though it took place six weeks ago. I feel more aware of my own vulnerability, and question what experiences I must have had in early childhood to leave such indelible feeling of desertion and loneliness. I greatly value my fantasy experience.

There is little to add to this moving account. During the fantasy, Sally physically went through all of the emotions she records: laughing, crying, tension, exhilaration. I took my job as fantasy guide to be helping Sally integrate her heart with the rest of her being. From the symbolism in the fantasy and from what we had already learned of Sally in the group, one of her difficulties was managing her feelings of affection. If she could build sound bridges from her heart to the rest of her body perhaps her love feelings could be handled more realistically in relation to herself. The work that Sally did symbolically and physically (through her physical changes throughout the fantasy) was to begin to overcome the alienation she felt toward her love feelings. The fantasy had allowed her to experience symbolically an accomplishment—integrating her heart—that she had never before done, thus increasing her confidence that she could deal successfully with romantic feelings and situations.

Her struggle with loving and being loved goes on but, as she reports, it's different now. She feels more able to cope. Subsequent communication with Sally reveals far greater clarity in what she wants, both personally and professionally. She has made several major decisions, including a change in job about which she reports feeling very pleased and confident.

As these examples demonstrate, under the appropriate circumstances, the fantasy methods are extraordinarily powerful and effective. At their best they allow a person to identify his very deepest problems and symbolically to grapple with them. If the fight is successful, then, in a real sense, the individual has "dreamed the impossible dream," and now has a new image of himself. He is now a person who can do what he didn't think he could do. His potential is released, and joy and exhilaration emerge.

The methods designed to enhance personal functioning are aimed primarily at increasing awareness of the power and capacity within each person, unblocking the obstacles to full expression, and practicing and training to develop these abilities and to integrate them into total human functioning. Again the non-verbal methods play a central role in many of these techniques. In addition, the methods of fantasy, imagery, and dramatization are invaluable for increasing internal awareness. As mentioned earlier, the techniques presented by no means exhaust the many approaches to enhancing personal functioning, but they do present some sense of the possibilities, especially around the concept of creativity.

These methods, however, are not designed to deal with the potential for joy derived from human interaction. The next section is devoted to techniques aimed at enriching interpersonal relations.

4 • Interpersonal Relations

In an earlier publication,[1] I proposed the notion that there are three basic interpersonal needs. These needs form the basis for exploring the realm of interpersonal relations and the methods whereby full human potential may be achieved between man and man.

For many—perhaps most—people, the primary source of joy is other people. But joy implies the possibility of misery; where there is ecstasy, so is there agony; if hell is other people, so is the divine. The theory pinpoints the arenas of joy and misery as the interpersonal-need areas called *inclusion, control,* and *affection.*

Inclusion behavior refers to association between people, being excluded or included, belonging, togetherness. The need to be included manifests itself as wanting to be attended to, and to attract attention and interest. The classroom hellion who throws erasers is often objecting mostly to the lack of attention paid him. Even if he is given negative affection he is partially satisfied, because at least someone is paying attention to him.

Being a distinct person, that is, having an identity, is an essential aspect of inclusion. An integral part of being recognized and paid attention

---

[1] See footnote on page 21.

to is that the individual be distinguishable from other people. He must be known as a specific individual; he must have a particular identity. The extreme of this identification is that he be understood. To be understood implies that someone is interested enough in him to find out his particular characteristics.

An issue that arises frequently at the outset of interpersonal relations is that of commitment, the decision to become involved in a given relation or activity. Usually, in the initial testing of a relationship, individuals try to present themselves to one another, partly to find out in which facet of themselves others will be interested. Frequently, a member is initially silent because he is not sure that people are interested in him, a concern about inclusion.

The flavor of inclusion is conveyed through such concepts as interacting with people, with attention, acknowledgment, prominence, recognition, and prestige; with identity, individuality, and interest. It is unlike affection in that it does not involve strong emotional attachments to individual persons. It is unlike control in that the pre-occupation is with prominence, not dominance.

Control behavior refers to the decision-making process between people, and the areas of power, influence, and authority. The need for control varies along a continuum from the desire for power, authority, and control over others (and therefore over one's future), to the need to be controlled, and have responsibility lifted from oneself.

An argument provides the setting for distinguishing the inclusion-seeker from the control-seeker. The one seeking inclusion or prominence wants very much to be one of the participants in the argument, while the control-seeker wants to be the winner or, if not the winner, on the same side as the winner. The prominence-seeker would prefer to be the losing participant; the dominance-seeker would prefer to be a winning nonparticipant.

Control is also manifested in behavior directed toward people who try to control others. Expressions of independence and rebellion exemplify lack of willingness to be controlled, while compliance, submission, and taking orders indicate various degrees of accepting the control of others. There is no necessary relation between an individual's behavior toward controlling others and his behavior toward being controlled. Two persons who control others may differ in the degree to which they allow others to control them. The domineering sergeant, for example, may accept orders from his lieutenant with pleasure and gratefulness, while the neighborhood bully may also rebel against his parents.

Control behavior differs from inclusion behavior in that it does not require prominence. The "power behind the throne" is an excellent example of a role that would fill a high control-need and a low need for inclusion. The "joker" exemplifies a high inclusion-need and a low need for control. Control behavior differs from affection behavior in that it has to do with power relations rather than emotional closeness. The frequent difficulties between those who want to "get down to business" and those who want to get to "know one another" illustrate a situation in which control behavior is more important for some and affection behavior for others.

Affection behavior refers to close personal emotional feelings between two people, especially love and hate in their various degrees. Affection is a dyadic relation; it can occur only between pairs of people at any one time, whereas both inclusion and control relations may occur either in dyads or between one person and a group of persons.

In groups, affection behavior is characterized by overtures of friendship and differentiation between members. A common method of avoiding a close tie with any one member is to be equally friendly to all members. Thus, "popularity" may not involve affection at all; it may often be inclusion behavior, as contrasted with "going steady," which is usually primarily affection.

A difference between inclusion behavior, control behavior, and affection behavior is illustrated by the different feelings a man has in being turned down by a fraternity, failed in a course by a professor, and rejected by his girl. The fraternity excludes him, telling him that they as a group don't have sufficient interest in him. The professor fails him and says, in effect, that he finds him incompetent in his field. His girl rejects him, implying that she doesn't find him lovable.

With respect to an interpersonal relation, inclusion is concerned primarily with the formation of a relation, whereas control and affection are concerned with relations already formed. Within existent relations, control is the area concerned with who gives orders and makes decisions for whom, whereas affection is concerned with how emotionally close or distant the relation becomes. Inclusion is concerned with the problem of *in or out*, control is concerned with *top or bottom*, and affection with *close or far*.

The specific difficulties that arise in each area, and that must be overcome in order to realize the full potential of human relationships, are described below, along with techniques for dealing with these difficulties. Perhaps the simplest way of discussing these difficulties is to caricature a person who is overbalanced in these areas both in having too much and having too little of what he needs.

Inclusion

Since the inclusion area involves the process of formation, it usually occurs first in the life of a group. People must decide whether they do or don't want to form a group. The issues of interaction are those of making contact, or *encounter*.

A person who has too little inclusion, who will be called undersocial, tends to be introverted and withdrawn. Consciously, he wants to maintain this distance between himself and others, and insists that he doesn't want to get enmeshed with people and lose his privacy. But unconsciously, he definitely wants others to pay attention to him. His biggest fears are that people will ignore him, generally have no interest in him, and would just as soon leave him behind.

His unconscious attitude may be summarized by, "No one is interested in me, so I'm not going to risk being ignored. I'll stay away from people and get along by myself." There is a strong drive toward self-sufficiency as a technique for existence without others. Behind his withdrawal is the private feeling that others don't understand him.

His deepest anxiety, that referring to the self-concept, is that he is worthless. He thinks that if no one ever considered him important enough to receive attention, he must be of no value whatsoever (see Deborah, for example, page 92). It is likely that this basic fear of abandonment or isolation is the most potent of all interpersonal fears.

The oversocial person tends toward extraversion. He seeks people incessantly and wants them to seek him out. He is also afraid they will ignore him. His unconscious feelings are the same as those of the withdrawn person, but his overt behavior is the opposite.

His unconscious attitude is summarized by, "Although no one is interested in me, I'll make people pay attention to me in any way I can." His inclination is always to seek companionship. He is the type who "can't stand being alone." All of his activities will be designed to be done "together."

The interpersonal behavior of the oversocial type of person is designed to focus attention on himself, to make people notice him, to be prominent. The direct method is to be an intensive, exhibitionistic participator. By simply forcing himself on the group he forces the group to focus attention on him. The more subtle technique is to try to acquire power (control) or try to be well liked (affection), but for the primary purpose of gaining attention.

To the individual for whom the resolution of inclusion relations was successful in childhood, interaction with people presents no problem. He is comfortable with people and comfortable being alone. He can be a high or low participator in a group, or can take a moderate role equally well, without anxiety. He is capable of strong commitment to and involvement with certain groups and also can withhold commitment if he feels it is appropriate. Unconsciously, he feels that he is a worthwhile, significant person.

Several methods help to bring out inclusion feelings. They focus on the issue involving contact and human encounter, and help to clarify the feelings and lead to some effective coping methods.

MAKING CONTACT

When: One of the most widespread human problems of modern society is making contact with other humans. Painfully few methods for meeting are socially acceptable, a condition that makes for much human heartbreak. Furthermore, the discomfort in actually verbally engaging another person, in knowing "what to say," or what to do to prolong and develop the association, is a serious problem for far too many. The agony of this situation is underscored in the extremes found in psychotic patients, many of whom simply have not learned how to enter the human race, how to make contact with another person. When the issue is one of learning how to join with others, several methods have proven useful.[2]

---

[2] These and some of the other body-movement methods were introduced to me by Joyce and John Weir (California Institute of Technology). Others from whom I learned much were Robert Tannenbaum

Feeling Space. All members of the group are asked to gather close together, either sitting on the floor (which is preferable) or sitting on chairs. Then they are asked to close their eyes and, stretching out their hands, "feel their space"—all the space in front of them, over their heads, behind their backs, below them—and then be aware of their contact with others as they overlap and begin to touch each other. This procedure is allowed to continue for about five minutes. (Do it now, before reading further, for the best understanding.)

Usually there are a variety of clear reactions. Some people definitely prefer to stay in their own space and resent as an intrusion anyone coming into it. Others feel very chary about intruding themselves in others' space for fear that they are not wanted. Still others seek out people and enjoy the touch contact. Where one person is inviting, another may be forbidding and simply touch and run. Discussion following this activity is usually very valuable in opening up the whole area of feelings about aloneness and contact.

Blind Milling. Feeling space helps to open up the area of conflict between being alone and being together. A next step is to explore more fully the nature of the other people, still non-verbally. This can be done by having everyone stand up, shut

(UCLA School of Business), Gene Sagan (San Francisco), and Hannah Weiner. Some of the methods are being developed in the Personal Growth laboratories at the annual summer workshops of the National Training Laboratories at Bethel, Maine.

his eyes, put out his hands and just start milling around the room. When people meet they explore each other in whatever way and for however long they wish. Slow accompanying music often enhances this experience. (Try it now if you can.)

Frequently the feeling is more general than individualized. That is, the experience is more significant for encountering the generalized other —the group—than it is in contacting individuals. For that reason, this method frequently enhances cohesive ties within a group. Moreover, it often sharpens awareness of the other people as human beings. If some individuals seemed of little interest before the blind milling, their identity and interest as people seem to be enhanced after it.

Literal Representation. Using space and movement to help a person feel his behavior more keenly, especially inclusion behavior, is often a very helpful method. Where talking is simply *about* the feeling, acting it out usually leads to more meaningful confrontation. A highly verbal young psychiatrist in a group of psychiatric trainees was forced by the group to carry out physically what he was doing through his behavior in the group. The results were very valuable. He writes, "The incident I recall most intensely was the following: I had been asking the group to go further and deeper in its explorations of feelings toward one another, but was reluctant to be the first to jump in. Someone tried to encourage me to get up and confront another member toward whom I felt most negatively at the time. I could not do this, refused, and then was punitively told to leave the group and sit in the corner. This I could do. I then felt both physically and emotionally isolated. I shook to the center of my being with the realization that I would rather withdraw than confront another person directly. I remember tears welling up as I saw the role I played in my own loneliness."

Bumping. Another instance of using a physical representation of an emotional state occurred when a man was talking about not feeling enough a part of the group. A method for sharpening his feeling occurred when he used the term "bumping." Here is Harold's description of what happened.

Harold's account: My participation up to this time had been fairly satisfying. I had interacted with several individuals on a rather significant basis. However, subconsciously I was wondering about my real importance to the group; I had not been "dealt with" by the whole group.

At this particular session I was feeling a growing frustration and disappointment in an attempt to communicate with one fellow. I was beginning to feel resentment toward him because he didn't seem to understand my questions and suggestions regarding his previous behavior and was turning the interrogation back onto me. Then people began to ask about my feelings and to draw inferences about them and I was feeling pressured and my resentment was rising. At the same time I was enjoying being the center of attention, and said that I felt for the first time I was "bumping up against people," and that I liked it, even though I had some negative feelings.

The suggestion was made for the men in the

group to form a close circle with me in the center, bumping them shoulder-to-shoulder in "rooster-fight" fashion, I said it would be very important for them to bump me back, otherwise it wouldn't be a real encounter. So we began, and the bumping increased in intensity. I felt free to attack the other men and they returned the bumping in kind, for three or four vigorous minutes.

It felt good. Solid. Real. Power. Encounter. Release. Satisfaction with myself. Comradely toward the fellows. We had met. The fight was over. I was in. I was caught up in a feeling of exhilaration.

I took my seat again beside the fellow I had tried to communicate with. I no longer really cared what he thought about me, or whether or not he wanted to pursue what I was trying to say to him. I chuckled and told him he could go to hell. I was half kidding. But I felt ten times stronger and more a part of things. I had established a deeper relationship with the group; it was one more step in my growing freedom and ability to relate with other people at a deeper level of mutual interaction.

Obviously, this type of activity did not completely resolve Harold's feeling of insignificance, but it may be of considerable help in starting him on the road to dealing with this feeling more effectively.

First Impression. Specifically focusing on another individual while using many senses helps a person to make contact. Ordinarily we are either oblivious to many cues the other person gives or we are reacting to them unconsciously rather than consciously. One way of exploring these cues is to begin a new group by having each member stand in front of the whole group. The group is instructed to give a first impression, perhaps a few adjectives, based entirely on appearance, preferably even before the person speaks. "Watch the structure of the body, the way the body is held, look carefully at the expression on the face, at the way he moves, at the tension and relaxation reflected in movement and positioning. Then go up and touch him, note the feel of the skin—the firmness or softness; the size, firmness and tension of the muscles; the quality of the hair. Now push him or have him push you and see the resistance or compliance. Then add more adjectives or reinforce or amend the first ones. Now smell him." How rarely we deliberately use smell, but it is often the repository of memories (who can forget the Prom gardenia smell?), and may affect or impress in a way of which we are not aware.

After this first contact, group members may be allowed some time together, perhaps half an hour, and then be asked to continue giving their first impressions. This time several new features are added. First, group members are brought into direct interaction with each other. Each person is asked to give his first impression of each of the other group members, not only verbally, but by standing directly in front of the person to get a much more direct awareness of his presence, looking him straight in the eye so that his attention is more easily directed to the person, and touching him in whatever way best expresses the toucher's feelings while he describes his impression. This procedure makes the reality of the other person much greater.

This experience is usually a very emotionally involving one for both the teller and the told, and typically brings the group members much closer together. Often there is resistance to the touching. This follows from the meaning given to it in our society, which interprets touch as basically aggressive or sexual. Such an interpretation, of course, need not be the case, but it does prevent warmer direct expression of feeling. A group context can frequently release people to feel more comfortable about touching. If the resistance to actual contact is too great, a person may give his impression without touching.

In all of these methods the inclusion problem is highlighted. How does one relate to people and what are the feelings involved? Another societal bar to real contact is the stereotypes we apply to each other, and the expectations that sometimes entrap people into limited acceptable modes of behavior. The next method usually alleviates this problem.

NEW NAMES

When: Before a group begins, if members are not previously acquainted, a valuable opportunity exists for the members to shed the expectations accrued from their past identities by taking new names and by agreeing not to talk about their backgrounds—occupation, home town, etc.—at least at the beginning of the group. Sometimes the trappings of a job, such as clergyman, psychiatrist, nurse, teacher, business executive, require certain types of behavior and elicit stereotyped responses. Under such an agreement an individual is able to explore himself more fully by seeing how he really would act and feel outside of his occupational constraints and how people would react to him as a person rather than as a member of a specific group.

How: Before they have an opportunity to know each other, group members are given new names, and these are the only names by which they are to be known throughout the life of the group. Usually only a first name is used. Several ways of assigning names are possible. A list of male and female names may be made up and each person assigned a name randomly. Or each person may be placed before the group and various suggestions made by the group members until one name satisfies both the individual and the group. Or each person may choose a name that connotes something to which he aspires. The latter two methods seem to be the most successful, although group members are free to select any method they wish.

Frequently, certain people will want to change their names during the group's life, or change back to their real names eventually, or at some point will want to reveal their true identity or want to know that of someone else. People are free to do any of these things since the desires usually stem from a considered exploration, or from an excess of anxiety, rather than from stereotyped, conventional thinking.

Caution: Seriously disturbed people with identity problems, very rigid people, and assorted others, for unclear reasons, sometimes have difficulty giving up their own names. In these cases it is best to let them retain their own names.

Examples: Some of the most useful name changes were the following. A rather dowdy-looking, middle-aged, plump, school psychologist was named Henrietta. She asked the group to give her a name that was just the opposite of the way she looked because at this point in her life she wasn't very happy with herself. The group finally settled on "Bubbles," a name that delighted her. She gradually began to feel a little freer as she became more comfortable with "Bubbles," but the name change was not sufficient to effect a significant behavior alteration. She was still stiff and subdued enough for one member of the group to say that sometimes he felt like shaking her. Following the principle of converting feelings into actions, he was asked if he would actually do it. He got up, took Bubbles by the shoulders and shook her up and down until they were bouncing all over the room with tremendous vigor. Bubbles began to effervesce. Her face was ruddy, and she glowed. She was literally bubbly. A side of her that had never shown began to emerge. She was very cute, frisky, mischievous, and she excelled at repartee. This pattern continued as she became more and more adventurous in the behavior she was willing to try. At the end of the lab she was exuberant and actually made attempts back at work, for the first few weeks, to have people call her "Bubbles."

In this group there was also a small, pixie-like man who seemed to get a huge delight out of all the group events, especially some of the movement and dance activities. This was so characteristic

that he accepted the name of "Pix." His delight
with the name helped him to continue his sprightly
behavior. He was particularly interested in being
with the female members of the group, especially
the pretty ones. His gay, abandoned behavior
captivated everyone. Toward the end of the workshop a rumor started that he was a priest. Someone mentioned the rumor, and he acknowledged
that he was a Roman Catholic priest, and had been
one for thirty-five years. The group was startled.
This certainly didn't fit their stereotype.

What happened: After the experience, Pix expressed his deep appreciation for the opportunity
to keep his identity unknown. It was the first time
in thirty-five years that he could learn how people
responded to him as a human being and not as a
priest. And he had a chance to express some of the
feelings he had been suppressing. As he spoke,
tears welled up in his eyes and his gratitude overwhelmed him. Many group members spontaneously
embraced him, and he hugged them back tightly.
This moving scene left Pix with a warm, glowing
smile which he retained for the remainder of the
group life. He vowed to go back and try to
influence his church to experience more of the
warmth and humanness that he experienced.
Many months later the glow had not diminished,
and he seemed to return to his job with added
strength and confidence about the person under
his robes.

For some people, like Bubbles and Pix, this
experience is like getting another chance in life,
by throwing off the background that has narrowed
the opportunity for growth. Both of them were

able to take full advantage of the opportunity and felt a strong feeling of self-renewal.

The next method deals with the problem of alienation felt so widely in this society. In virtually every encounter group some feel it as a major problem. This technique again uses the principle of doing rather than only verbalizing.

BREAK IN

When: In any social setting, the concepts of alienation, isolation, and loneliness have a prominent part. The feeling of being excluded from a group, or not being in the most desirable group, or not being a full-fledged member, is a feeling shared by most of mankind. It is such a sharp, uncomfortable feeling that it becomes subject to much denial and distortion. When the topic is raised sharply in a group, the procedure of *breaking in* is often useful as a direct confrontation of the feelings of inclusion for both the "ins" and those trying to gain entrance.

How: The people identified as "in" stand and form a tight circle with interlocking arms. They may face either inward or outward depending upon whether the person trying to break in sees them as simply involved with each other and ignoring him (face in), or as deliberately attempting to keep him out (face out). The outsider then tries to break through into the circle in whatever way he can, and the group members try to keep him out. Another variation is to have the outsider try to break the circle and take his place alongside the others as a regular member. Which goal he aspires to is left to the outsider.

Usually there is discussion afterwards. It often happens that some of the other people also want to try to break in since this activity often elicits great empathy.

Caution: Breaking in can become quite violent, so that heart or other physical disabilities that may be endangered by strong physical activity should disqualify someone from this exercise. Also, care should be taken that there is no breakable furniture within several feet of the group and no sharp objects against which people could be thrown and hurt.

Example: At a lecture-demonstration of some of these methods, one girl complained that she wasn't understanding or getting as much from them as others who were already familiar with the techniques. They seemed to dominate the discussions and appeared to know more.

She was asked to step up front and pick out five or six of these people, which she promptly did. They then formed an inward circle and she was asked to break in. She walked slowly about the circle and made a few abortive attempts to pull two people apart. Then she concentrated on the strongest male in the group and worked for several minutes trying to break his grip on his partner, finally giving up this obviously futile attempt. After continuing to poke at various points in the group she decided to stop, and said that she really didn't care that much about being in the group anyway.

This performance infuriated two members of the audience. One could barely contain himself. He said he couldn't understand how she could be so casual about the situation. As soon as she began he had immediately pictured himself in the situation and imagined kicking, or clawing, or smashing, or doing anything to break into the group. The mere idea of the group members keeping him out was enough to almost enrage him.

Another observer wanted a chance to break in. He had apparently been thinking a lot about it and mapped his strategy. He circled the group slowly, apparently testing for weak spots. Then he began to tickle several of the members until he found one who was ticklish. He tickled her, she released her grip, and *voila!* he was in.

What happened: Subsequent investigation revealed how typical the three different approaches were of the three people involved. The first girl's approach of trying half-heartedly, silently asking to be let in without actually committing herself to making the request, and then rationalizing the whole situation as one she didn't care about anyway, apparently typified her relations to things she really wanted. It helped explain why she often found herself on the outside and denied the things she wanted. Her behavior made this characteristic very clear to everyone, including herself, and pointed up the difficulties of expressing her needs directly, her demands on others to anticipate her needs, and her defensive reaction to rejection by asserting that she didn't care.

The imagined violent reaction of the second man, a college professor, also surprised him greatly. His immediate feelings of violence underscored for him his strong reaction to being excluded, a feeling he could trace back to being a minority-group member, among other things. But the residue of unresolved anger from those early experiences was startling for him to experience.

The use of guile by the third breaker-in also clarified his style to him and those who knew him. Characteristically, he tested a situation to find its vulnerable points and then entered at the weakest point, without the group even feeling that it had been penetrated. The reaction of various group members also helped him to understand various reactions he had received at other points in his life. Some were very admiring of his tactic. Others were quite angry, especially the men, since they felt that he had sneaked in and hadn't really earned what he had achieved.

In each case the style of dealing with exclusion was clearly revealed by this simple situation. Such a revelation may lead to a much greater understanding of the person's mode of dealing with exclusion. Also the feelings of the people in the circle emerge clearly, some being in conflict and only trying half-heartedly, while others feel strongly and try vociferously to exclude.

The pattern of inclusion or exclusion for the group as a whole is given by the next method.

MILLING

When: Knowing the structure of the group itself is frequently important for determining the needs of various members. If, for example, some members feel isolated, it is helpful to bring this fact to the attention of the rest. Often, talking about issues of this type doesn't clarify the situation because people may not know or be willing to admit their feelings, for example, that they feel alienated from the group. Milling is a way of clarifying these issues.

How: The leader of the group stands up, moves a few feet away from the group, and states, "I would like you to get up, one at a time, and walk toward me and keep walking in any direction you want. Stop wherever you feel most comfortable. Don't try to figure out where you want to be. Just let your body lead you to where it wants to go. If you don't feel like settling, keep milling around. When others come near, you may feel like turning, moving away, moving toward them, or staying still. Do what you feel. We will just continue milling until everyone is located somewhere, or is constantly moving." The group leader follows his own instructions. When the group members have completed this task, they usually sit down and discuss the experience.

Sometimes groups are unable to move, but the value of the experience can be retained by asking for the wishes or fantasies that they had about what they would like to have done if they were able to move. It is very rare that anyone has no feelings about the experience.

Cautions: None.

Example: One member in a group of psychiatrists seemed to have fallen behind his peers. He had missed several meetings, his interest appeared to be waning, and his attention was intermittent. At the same time, the group was beginning to split on the issue of whether they should delve deeper into feelings, or keep their interaction on a more superficial level. Factors for and against the group leader, who favored more depth, seemed to be forming covertly. To try to clarify all these guessed-at phenomena, the leader suggested the milling activity and stood up. The members of the group all rose and stood behind their chairs; all, that is, except the alienated one, who stated that he felt more comfortable sitting. Even after several minutes of standing, none of the group members would move, so everyone sat down. The exercise appeared to be a failure. The group began to discuss why psychiatrists, with their very different orientation toward group work—that is, basically talking and rarely if ever moving—might find milling difficult. Then one of the members suggested that they tell what their fantasies were during their immobile minutes. He started by saying that he wanted desperately to hug the two people beside him, one male, one female, but something prevented it. Another member related how he wanted to run away from the group into the corner and look out the window all alone. Another wanted to go up to the leader and stand in front of him, and another wanted to hide his head. As the fantasies emerged, the group structure was clarified, even though the group had not been able to mill. These feelings were discussed at length during the next several meetings and the responses of members toward the group, the leader, and each other became much clearer.

What happened: This exercise, too, uses the whole body as a unit to reveal and clarify internal feelings, rather than leaving the feelings to be revealed through only thinking. The feelings revealed by tensions in the body provided the group members with much more information about their attitudes within the group. Even though they couldn't allow these feelings to move them physically, the feelings did register in their cognitive world where, by training and personality, the psychiatrists are more used to functioning. The group was able to use these realizations productively.

In these interpersonal exercises, not only are the feelings converted to movement, but advantage is taken of the feelings aroused by the proximity of two physical beings. Moving toward or away from a person is a clear indication of the feelings existing between the two. In everyday life this is obvious. If someone is attractive, the impulse is to hug and caress; if they are repulsive, the impulse is to leave; if they rouse anger, then hitting or pushing is the desire. In all cases the feelings are directly converted into some physical relationship. It then follows that if clarification of feelings is desired, testing for the comfortable physical distance is a key method.

The next three techniques are appropriate for improving the relation between two people. Frequently it is difficult for individuals to make contact, or to communicate adequately. These methods aid this process.

NON-VERBAL COMMUNICATION—DYAD

When: Often two people will try to express their feelings toward each other verbally, or will try to explain themselves or some situation, and they simply can't understand each other. This occurs when people are inarticulate, when conflicts about their feelings are prominent and they try to hide it, when actually they are not really familiar with what their feeling is, or when they are very intellectualized and the words are used defensively to obfuscate the situation. In any of these situations two approaches may be found helpful. The first one stays with verbal interaction and the second turns non-verbal. It is often most effective to use first one, then the other, in that order.

How: In the first method each participant is asked to stop talking and to try to state his adversary's position as clearly and sympathetically as possible. Often, initial attempts mock the position. It is important to insist then that it be stated as if it were a reasonable position to take. This forces the protagonist to think of the cogency of his opponent's argument.

The second method for clarifying an interaction is to ask the two participants to continue to communicate, but without using words. The defensive, obscuring function of the words is eliminated and the feelings are directed away from the head, down toward the body. Some people find this difficult in that they feel inhibited in moving. The benefit of the method can still be maintained by asking what fantasies or pictures immediately came to mind. People usually have an immediate impulse which they can identify.

In both methods it is very helpful to first ask the adversaries to sit facing each other. The direct physical confrontation makes the situation more real and involving than it is when the two people sit at a long distance from each other.

Caution: No special cautions are connected with this experience. There may be a slightly increased tendency toward physical violence because of the physical proximity but no violence has ever happened in my experience.

Example: In a group of businessmen there was a strong unresolved problem between two of the participants. Their only interaction had been sniping and making rather snide asides in response to each other's contributions. Finally the rest of the group encouraged the two to engage each other to uncover what was going on, since it made the other group members uncomfortable. They began to talk at great length to no avail. Then they were asked to sit next to each other, which they did with no hesitation. They continued to talk and some group members tried to help clarify their difficulty but it seemed that the more they talked, the more unclear the situation became. When requested to repeat the other's position they were unable to comply because neither position was sufficiently clear.

At this point they were asked to continue without words, and one of them immediately took the other one and put him on his lap. Instantly the situation became clear. The lap-sitter got off and said that that was exactly the problem. He felt patronized and treated like a child and he resented it. The other agreed that he felt that way and that he did see him as very dependent and childlike, and not acting like an adult. The ensuing communication was very relevant and they began to make progress toward a resolution. Also, the others were able to add their own observations and impressions now that the issue was clear. Where the verbalizing had made the matter obscure by trying to relive specific situations and justify specific previous interactions, the non-verbal communication had gotten to the basic core of the difficulty. When that was revealed, the problem was obvious to the participants.

One further example may illuminate another advantage of sometimes eliminating words. A man and a woman were exchanging very hostile comments in the group and again apparently getting nowhere. The woman was very angry, critical and attacking. He, in turn, was defending himself and occasionally counterattacking. When asked to stop talking but to continue to communicate, to everyone's surprise, including their own, they both stood up, the woman immediately went over to the man who put out his arms to receive her, and they had a long and warm embrace. In the subsequent discussion the affection between them came to light along with the fear that their affection was unreciprocated. The woman felt that he didn't like her and she was very angry and bitter about this and took every opportunity to get even. When their real feelings came through, the need for the attack and defense was eliminated. They did, in fact, like each other, the sharpness disappeared, and they began building a closer, more supportive relationship. Here the verbalizing was not just obscuring the issue as in the first example, but it was conveying the very opposite of the true situation. The behavior was hostility but the underlying feeling was affection along with fear.

What happened: Especially with intellectual people, words paradoxically can be the largest obstacle to communication. People often spend a great deal of time and words trying *not* to say something like, "You're too childish," or avoiding the central point, which is often unknown to themselves, as in the second example. When they are suddenly stripped of their verbal defense it is as if their outer layer is taken off, revealing the feeling that is being defended against, patronizing-dependency in the first example, and affection-resentment at unreciprocation in the second. Relieving people of the burden of using words allows the real feelings to surface. When the feelings are clarified, continued verbalizing can be used productively because it is about present feelings and loses its defensive quality.

One point should be made clear. Verbalizing is not always defensive. The type of verbalizing that follows a non-verbal clarification is usually of a totally different nature and should be encouraged as long as it helps to work out present feelings. There is a danger here too, however. Sometimes talking about a just completed dramatic non-verbal incident continues beyond the time it is productive and begins to have a defensive quality of a different nature, namely, that of trying to talk away the experience. The incident may have stirred up strong feelings which are somewhat unfamiliar to the individuals and difficult for them to handle. One way of dealing with the feelings is to talk them to death so that they disappear. It is usually obvious when this occurs because the discussion becomes boring and people stop listening. The non-verbal event was involving and now the talk seems like repetitious chatter.

A more direct and usually stronger approach to this issue of attaining direct and satisfactory contact between people is provided by the next method.

THE ENCOUNTER

When: Words are special culprits in the effort to avoid real personal confrontation. At times, when a real communication should be established, it may be necessary to cut through words and other defensive activities and to help the participants become aware of their real response toward each other again through the use of feelings in their whole body.

How: The two persons involved are asked to stand at opposite ends of the room. They are instructed to remain silent, look into each other's eyes, and walk very slowly toward each other. Without planning anything, when the two people get close to each other, they are to do whatever they are impelled from within themselves to do. They are to continue to encounter for as long as they wish. After it is completed the principals will ordinarily talk about their feelings, and the others will contribute their observations and identifications with the principals. It is essential to urge the principals to try to let their feelings take over and not plan what they will do when they meet. (Try it now before reading on if you have a companion.) Many variations appear and should be noted, such as which person wants to leave first, how uncomfortable each feels, if they embrace whether it is a warm feeling or a way of avoiding looking at each other, who initiates the action, and so on.

Caution: There are no special problems with this experience. It can be very revealing and unsettling, but people usually know whether or not they are ready for it.

Example: George had just been divorced and appeared to have much hostility as well as great attraction toward women. His feelings about women were apparently very confused, but he treated the whole area flippantly and with many jokes. Marla was very attractive and had very ambivalent feelings toward men. She was very dependent on them on the one hand, and very competitive on the other. She and George had avoided each other in the group until someone remarked that their feelings toward the opposite sex seemed similar and wondered how they felt about each other. Characteristically neither could identify or verbalize how they actually felt toward the other. They said that they didn't feel anything. It seemed like an appropriate time for an encounter since it might allow them to become aware of their feelings toward each other that were being blocked inside them. They approached each other slowly and when they met, George looked at Marla briefly and walked right by her, staring straight ahead. For fully five minutes both stood still, backs to each other, looking in opposite directions. The tension became too great for the observers and they began to urge the principals on to various resolutions of the impasse, but George and Marla accepted none. Then Marla stepped back, took George by the shoulders and turned him around so that she was facing his back. She then stepped back and the group waited anxiously for the next move. They didn't have to wait long, for Marla stepped up and delivered a tremendous kick in the rear to George, knocking him several feet across the room. Stunned, George just looked at Marla, who then invited him to kick her back.

He refused until she finally took a pillow and put it behind her. Reluctantly, George kicked her, but gently.

The effect of this interchange was different for the two participants. Marla felt elated and strong, her participation increased, and she became softer. Later, in a psychodrama, she was able to work on her relation to her father, which helped clarify her feelings toward men. George became depressed. His difficulties with women were serious and he was forced to face them directly, something he had successfully avoided up to that time. *What happened:* The encounter allowed Marla to experience one of her most basic fears, male rejection, blatant and unmistakable—a man looked at her, walked away, and turned his back. She found the strength to deal with the situation however, by expressing the anger and hurt most directly, and then being able to show compassion and fairness. She had coped successfully with a very frightening situation and felt the exhilaration of her success. The softness felt later was the femininity that could come through now that men didn't have to be attacked out of her fear of being rejected by them. For George, the encounter confronted him starkly with the severity of his problem and tore away his frivolous exterior. He couldn't feel much for a woman and what he did feel was anger. He couldn't fake jocular feelings in the encounter, and he was forced to feel—literally—the effect of his behavior on the woman. In subsequent meetings he settled down to working on the problem. In both cases the encounter stripped away the verbalization and presented the problem in its most basic terms, allowing in one case a partial resolution and in the other a more realistic inspection.

The fantasy methods that are of such great value for individuals can be adapted to group problems.

GROUP FANTASY

How: There are several ways in which fantasies for more than one person may be generated. The following is the method so far found most productive. The fantasy begins with two or three of the people most involved with each other. They are asked to lie down on the floor on their backs with their heads together and their bodies stretched out like spokes on a wheel. This position is very restful and relaxing and puts the participants in a position to hear each other even when they speak softly. All members of the group are then asked to shut their eyes. One of the participants on the floor begins by relating whatever picture comes into his head, or someone may start him off with a specific image. Everyone else tries to enter his fantasy and carry it on in whatever way it happens inside the head. That is, it is not an attempt to consciously and deliberately make up a continuing story, but rather an attempt to have several people share the same fantasy.

Each person on the floor is to enter verbally at any time, whenever he wishes to, so that the fantasy continues. The other group members are asked to follow with the fantasy in their own imagination, and if they wish to enter they are to get down on the floor and join in verbally just as the others have been doing. If a participant is finished, he simply gets up from the floor and goes back to his regular place. The fantasy stops when participants want to stop. The group leader may enter toward the end and attempt to help the individuals finish with a satisfied feeling before asking them to open their eyes.

Frequently the group fantasy is a very moving experience. People may not want to talk immediately after it is over. If the fantasy goes well, the participants have actually been living in the fantasy, and they sometimes take a while to return.

Examples: Two examples will help to describe the use of a group fantasy to elicit and clarify two types of feeling, hostility and affection.

During the planning of a workshop involving the use of some of these methods, two members of the staff were having trouble dealing with each other, and identifying their difficulty. It was decided to use a group fantasy to help ease the situation. They began by imagining themselves in physical combat, an image suggested to them as a way of exploring their hostile feelings. They were quite able to enter the same fantasy most of the time, reporting how they wrestled each other to the ground, picked up a stick, rolled down a hill locked in each other's arms. There was a difficulty when one said he saw the other hitting him. The other couldn't see himself delivering the blow. This tension grew stronger and stronger, and finally both had to open their eyes and come out of the fantasy. Both looked and felt very agitated and nervous. They talked of the intense destructive impulses that began to appear as they had to share each other's fantasy and the strength of these impulses was too frightening.

It would not be a good idea to stop the fantasy at this point because apparently impulses have been uncovered which need some resolution. This is one type of situation which makes it unwise for an untrained person to use this method.

The two were put back into the fantasy and, through guidance by a third person, they began to turn toward a reconciliation. They opened their eyes and felt much better about each other for reasons neither understood at this time. Here is the fantasy as reported by each participant.

Jim's account: It seemed that the way the fantasy started was that the staff was confused as to what a group fantasy would involve, and Khrishna and Pierre were asked to act it out. My perception of that situation was that Pierre had picked up a stick and was trying to hit Khrishna with it. Khrishna refused to enter into the fantasy and he was avoiding being hit back by the stick that Pierre was wielding.

I felt very, very disgruntled and became quite angry with the way the fantasy was going. There was a transition and I got into the fantasy with Pierre and wanted very much to hit and maul him. The fantasy began with us wrestling and locked in that kind of an embrace which was furious in its energy and yet somehow safe in that we both had good grips on each other's arms and weren't hurting each other but merely pushing and shoving, and twisting each other around in a circle. Somehow then in the fantasy we rolled down a hill and hit a tree. In fact, I think I brought the tree in to resist a direction from you that we should end the struggle by rolling down the hill and falling into the river. At any rate the tree served the purpose of separating us and I distinctly remember being in a crouched position, almost catlike, and ready to pounce on Pierre, but not with a desire to lock arms again in the same kind of struggle that we had been engaged in previously, but to literally destroy him. It was at this point that the fantasy ended and we were asked to report to the group what it felt like. I was impressed with two things; the physical feeling of rage was very real and my heart was pounding; I was really feeling deprived and incomplete at the time that we had been brought out of the fantasy. The second thing was that the rest of the staff, a group of professionals who had witnessed people in interpersonal combat before, were also very much involved and not only absorbed in what was going on, but rooting for one or the other of the combatants and having fantasies themselves which privately accompanied the "main fantasy." Some of them were the kind which took the form of yelling to one of the participants to "look out," or I remember particularly Ron's, where he was yelling to Pierre to jump into the river and swim for it. Also the fantasy of one of the others who was yelling to Pierre to look for the stick that he had previously had in his hands, and to pick it up and beat me with it. Although Pierre and I were in the "main fantasy," in that the total group was being told what we were experiencing with each other through our verbal reports, there were several private fantasies in which all of the other members had entered into our fantasy and were observing us. This observation became so real for them that we spent quite a few minutes talking about our amazement at the strength of the hostility that was actually experienced by every member of the staff of ten people.

After we had talked for a while, Pierre and I went back into the fantasy and this time were told to picture ourselves seated by the river with our feet in the water, talking to each other. It became very easy then in the fantasy to explore some of the good feelings that Pierre and I had for each other. This didn't mean a great liking for each other but rather the ability for each of us to differentiate more clearly between the positive and negative aspects of the other in such a way that allowed us to appreciate one without accepting the other. In fact, after the fantasy, Pierre was able to say to me that his perception of me had always been one of a big mouth. But because of the fantasy he had gotten a better idea of who I was as a total person, and although the big-mouth aspect still irked him, it didn't block him from being able to speak to me honestly and use me as a resource in areas where he thought I could be helpful to him.

For me, the experience was frightening. It put me in touch with a strong feeling of wanting to destroy others, but the manner of destruction was one of mutilation rather than just shooting them with a bullet. It involved me very physically tearing the other person apart. The strength of that feeling has since then put a red flag on some of my interpersonal relations. I used to, many times, find myself verbally going in and hurting other people quite viciously and unintentionally or unconsciously. Today I feel I am not completely successful but at least better able to understand that I am somehow responding to this internal force rather than to the situation that I am involved in. In the past, this would result in the kind of a bind that's best exemplified by me trying to explain something to someone or to discuss something with them, and I begin to feel them pulling away from me at a point when I cannot really experience why they are pulling away from me. My response to their leaving me psychologically is for me to go after them more strongly, which is self-defeating since all they do is withdraw even more rapidly. My previous reaction to this would be to give full vent to the hostility and anger that I was experiencing and blame it completely on the person with whom I was involved. Now, since that fantasy, as well as several others in which I was put in touch with this feeling even more clearly, I stop whatever it is that I am doing and try, as honestly as I possibly can, to say to the other person: "I don't feel I'm being very fair with you," or something to that effect, which lets him know that I feel that a bit of irrationality has exhibited itself and it has really confused the issues that we were discussing.

Another important lesson from that fantasy is that I no longer fear that irrational side of me. I know it is there and I also know that there is enough sanity to not be afraid to give full vent to that irrational part of me, since it does two things: it gives me clearer handles as to where it came from, as well as giving the other person an opportunity to be able to cope with me more as a total person in a "more beneficial way" to both of us. Somehow that experience gave me an opportunity to work even more deeply with succeeding fantasies and to really allow the fantasy to take over as completely as it could. I feel that in a way my fantasies with male figures end up with me acting out a lot of the hostility that resulted toward my father, and yet that particular fantasy was the start of something which has continued to give me further insights into myself and to a lot of the emotion that influences my response to people on what I thought were non-emotional issues.

Pierre's account: I think the joint fantasy with Jim helped me to experience the amount of aggression I had within myself, but also feel, at a very primitive level, that it was neither dangerous nor "bad" to be aggressive. Before this experience, Jim had annoyed me a lot by what I was calling internally his "childish greediness." During the experience, I felt he was frail, and towards the end I discovered that what I was hating in him was also in me, and I felt good about him and with him. During the two weeks of the workshop we became quite good friends.

The second example occurred in a group that could not get started. The only bit of action that seemed to be happening in the group was a subtle attraction between a middle-aged man, Henry, and a woman, June. As a way of exploring this relation and of perhaps giving the group an important mutual experience that might help them come together, a group fantasy was suggested, to be begun by these two. They agreed, lay down on the floor, and began.

They pictured a house on top of a hill. June was in the large, beautiful kitchen, and Henry was many miles away down the hill. Though they wanted him to go to the house, their fantasies wouldn't take him there. Finally, the fantasy of one group member, as he followed along, started to diverge from that of Henry and June, so he slid down onto the floor and joined in. He saw himself riding up toward the house on a black horse, getting Henry, and taking him into the house with him. This image was viable for the other two and for the next several minutes they were all together in the house until it became clear that although they liked the man on the black horse, they didn't want him around. He gradually felt the same way and soon faded from the fantasy, got up from the floor and resumed his seat, his job having been completed.

The couple then wanted to go to the bedroom together, but again their fantasies wouldn't go in that direction. Henry finally left the house and June went into the backyard to garden. Eventually Henry returned, they began to talk, warm feelings arose with them, and they both felt that they could go to the bedroom any time they wished. They opened their eyes, embraced warmly, and felt extremely good about the experience and about each other.

Following is the experience as reported by Henry.

Henry's account: At the time I was asked to participate in the fantasy, I had a feeling of defensiveness, as I did not know what I might reveal of myself. This feeling was compounded when June was also asked to participate because of the previous connection that had been established in the group between us. However, I felt that I was in the group to learn and for this reason I did participate.

For a few minutes after I lay down and closed my eyes, I was very cognizant of the group being present and also that June was lying head-to-head with me. But as I entered into the fantasy which concerned the house that June and I found ourselves in, the presence of the people surrounding me disappeared and the only two people I was involved with were June and myself. This situation became more involved as a third party was injected into the fantasy, and I found myself wanting to get rid of the third party but wanting to do it without hurting him. If you will remember, the third party was finally dismissed from the fantasy and left June and me alone. During the fantasy, as June and I were involved in the kitchen and we started to walk from the kitchen down the hallway, I found myself in conflict with the desire to reach the end of the hall and the bedroom and a subconscious realization that I had no business doing it. At this point I saw a barrier in the middle of the hallway and June and I moved away from each other. She went out one door of the house and I went out the other. The interesting thing was that she went to the back of the house to plant flowers and I went around the house to meet her and then we approached the door of the house and entered into the kitchen again. This time there was no hesitation about the feeling between the two of us and we moved out of the kitchen and down the hallway towards the culmination of, I believe, the point of our desires. It was at this point that June jumped up and said (and I can remember this very vividly), "What I see about to happen is too beautiful to be shared with the rest of the group."

When June left me on the floor I felt like a person who had been left dangling on the edge of a cliff with almost no way of rescue. This is when I suddenly realized that a lot of things had happened in the fantasy which I had avoided, and this got me to asking myself, was I avoiding conflict in things other than in the fantasy? Of course, the fact that I was so emotionally involved made this experience a very vivid and living thing for me. I think, if you will remember, that I cried for about an hour. It wasn't until two days later that I really got control of myself. A postscript to the fantasy was that June and I had a talk after it was all over about her problems and some of mine, and we found consolation in knowing that we both had problems but that we could do something about them if we would face them.

I hope that this is the kind of a description of this experience that you wanted. By going into the blow-by-blow description of the fantasy I think it gives an overall picture of the type of emotional experience that it was for me. I would say that it was the most emotional experience that I have ever had in my life and that I will never forget it. It still lives with me in detail every day.

Following this, when I returned home, I had a confrontation with my wife and we ironed out a number of things that I had been avoiding talking about. In addition, the same thing happened when I returned to the office and I had a confrontation with my coordinate and boss and likewise confronted some of the things that I had been avoiding.

What happened: The mechanism through which the group fantasy operates is still relatively unknown. Apparently it is similar to communicating with a different level of awareness, with the unconscious. It frequently leaves the participants with very close feelings for each other without any intellectual understanding of why this is so. It also operates out of the control of the fantasizers, as illustrated in the two examples. In the first, the participants certainly had no desire to let their destructive impulses take over, but they did. In the second, there was a desire to go to bed together but the fantasy wouldn't "permit" it until the relation was developed further. The fantasy usually reveals what the underlying situation involves, and there is virtually always a complete acceptance by the fantasizer of the feelings described in the fantasy. In group, as in individual fantasies, there are marked physiological changes as the fantasy develops. In addition to the usual tension, worry, relaxation, crying, laughing, and other individual reactions, there are frequently instances of touching each other, either grasping for support or contact, or just a feeling for the other's presence.

The amount of identification by other group members is usually very great. There is much to be learned about the group fantasy but it is a very exciting and potentially even more valuable experience.

In summary, the methods used to clarify the inclusion area concentrate on the human encounter. By involving bodily feelings and fantasy-level productions, these methods help to make clearer the feelings people have for each other, especially about the amount of contact with which they feel comfortable. Most of the methods also provide an opportunity to pursue the process of engaging with people more tenaciously than most of us customarily do. If the pursuit of this contact is a positive experience it can lead to an increase in one's feeling of personal significance, and in confidence regarding one's ability to succeed at making connections with people. One can then proceed to enjoy more the human encounter.

The area of control is usually the next phase of the development of a human relation. Physical methods of a more vigorous and confronting type are valuable for dealing with these feelings.

Control

Control problems usually follow those of inclusion in the development of a group, or of an interpersonal relation. Once the group has formed, it begins to differentiate, different people take or seek different roles, and often power struggles, competition, and influence become central issues. In terms of interaction these are matters of *confrontation*.

The extreme person too low on control, an "abdicrat," is one who tends toward submission and abdication of power and responsibility in his interpersonal behavior. He gravitates toward the subordinate position where he will not have to take responsibility for making decisions, and where someone else takes charge. Consciously, he wants people to relieve him of his obligations. He does not control others even when he should; for example, he would not take charge even during a fire in a children's schoolhouse in which he is the only adult. He never makes a decision if he can refer it to someone else. He fears that others will not help him when he requires it, and that he will be given more responsibility than he can handle. This kind of person is usually a follower, or at most a loyal lieutenant, but rarely the person who takes the responsibility for making the final decision.

Unconsciously, he has the feeling that he is incapable of responsible adult behavior and that others know it. His most comfortable response is to avoid situations in which he will feel helpless. He feels that he is incompetent and irresponsible. Behind this feeling is hostility and lack of trust toward those who might withhold assistance.

The "autocrat" is a person whose interpersonal behavior is dominating in the extreme. He desires a power hierarchy with himself at the top. He is the powerseeker, the competer. He is afraid people will not be influenced or controlled by him —that they will, in fact, dominate him.

Commonly, this need to control people is displaced into other areas. Intellectual or athletic superiority allows for considerable control, as does the more direct method of attaining political power. The underlying feelings are the same as for the abdicrat. Basically, the person feels he is not responsible or capable of discharging obligation and that this fact will be found out by others. He attempts to use every opportunity to disprove this feeling to others and to himself. His unconscious attitude may be summarized as, "No one thinks I can make decisions for myself, but I'll show them. I'm going to make all the decisions for everyone, always." Behind this feeling is a strong distrust that others may make decisions for him, and the feeling that they don't trust him.

For the individual who has successfully resolved his relations with others in the control area in childhood, power and control present no problem. He feels comfortable giving or not giving orders, and taking or not taking orders, as is appropriate to the situation. Unconsciously, he feels that he is a capable, responsible person and therefore that he does not need to shrink from responsibility or to try constantly to prove how competent he really is. Unlike the abdicrat and autocrat, he is not preoccupied with fears of his own helplessness, stupidity, and incompetence. He feels that other people respect his competence and will be realistic with respect to trusting him with decision-making.

The needs in the control area can be dealt with effectively by several non-verbal techniques, and some applications of group fantasy. One of the simplest ways of bringing out feelings about the control situation is to experience the different power-relations spatially. To experience being dominant, a person stands on a chair and continues interacting from that position. The person in the chair has the experience of being subordinated. Also someone can sit on the floor while everyone else is seated, or remain seated while everyone else stands on chairs, and so forth. It is quite remarkable how these simple spatial changes bring out definite feelings of comfort or discomfort.

In addition to this initial introduction to the top-bottom feelings, there are several other ways in which control issues may be explored. Direct physical confrontation at various levels of strength is usually highly effective and to the point.

PHYSICAL CONFRONTATION

When: Interpersonal hostility and competition are emotions that are important to understand and handle well. However, society frowns strongly on their expression with the result that people devise a variety of techniques to hide these feelings from others as well as from themselves. It is often more effective to express hostility in a safe atmosphere. Then, direct ways of dealing with the feeling can be explored. Too often, the usual efforts to suppress these negative feelings lead to the suppression of the whole self. Following are some methods for bringing hostility and competition to the surface where they can be worked through.

How: Danish thumb-wrestling is a method for bringing out feelings of competition in a nonverbal direct confrontation which does not rely especially on strength. This technique is sometimes useful as a warm-up to more forceful encounters, but it can also be used alone for such situations as competition between a man and a woman. The two participants begin to shake hands but instead curl their four fingers and hook them into each other. This coupling must be held firmly throughout the match. The two thumbs are laid side by side, and then switch places by jumping over each other, three times. After they come to rest following the third switch they are quickly raised in combat, the objective being to "pin" the other thumb down so that it can't move for at least a count of three. It usually proves to be fun but gradually competitive feelings become aroused, especially in the person who loses.

Arm-wrestling is another common and ancient activity that is excellent for allowing two people to explore the power aspects of their relation. It is also one of the several activities that can be used to increase a person's involvement with a group. Lethargy fades and involvement is usually greatly increased when a person must mobilize his energies into a concerted physical effort. The arm-wrestle is usually best done by having the participants lie flat on the floor, put their right (or left) forearms up straight, leaning on the elbows, lock hands, put their elbows in a straight line between them, and then try to force the other man's arm to the ground without moving the elbow or using the other hand for support. Very often it is found that adult males are much closer in strength than appearance might indicate.

Probably the most complete exercise for exploring the power-dependency-competitive feelings between people is the Press.

The Press can help two people whose relation contains unresolved negative elements. The two individuals are asked to stand facing each other and are given the following instructions: "One of you place your hands on the other's shoulders and press him to the ground. You may use any method you wish to get him down but you must put him flat on his back on the ground. He may cooperate or resist or do whatever he wishes. After he is down, you are to help him to his feet. Again, he may help or resist depending on how he feels. When that is completed, reverse roles and do the same thing the other way."

After they have finished, the participants and the observers usually want to talk about their reactions. It is valuable to have reactions to all four aspects of the situation, the feeling of subduing, of helping someone you have subdued, of being subdued, and of being helped. Often one of these four experiences is much more salient than the other three. Frequently, there is much empathetic reaction from the observers, and these reactions are valuable to explore.

Caution: This may become a violent activity so anyone with heart or other physical disabilities should avoid it. There should be plenty of room available and protection from sharp or hard objects. Also, participants should remove glasses, watches, rings, earrings, etc., in case it becomes very physical. Most presses, however, are relatively calm.

Example: Mike was from a tough neighborhood and belonged to a minority ethnic group. He had made his way up through the academic world very successfully but he had paid a price. Apparently, his hostility had never been adequately expressed and he exuded a kind of Marlon Brando suppressed fury that could erupt at any time.

Along with this he seemed to have special problems with the female members of the group, at times being very warm, then cold and distant with them.

Ginny was a very competent, professional woman who was very verbal and charming, but who was quite threatening to several men in the group who saw her as competitive. She was hurt by this and expressed herself to the effect that that was their problem, not hers. She and Mike seemed to have a reasonably good relation but not one in which much closeness had been established, partly, perhaps, because it was still early in the group's life. The group was confronting Mike about his suppressed rage. He, in turn, was trying to talk about it, sometimes denying it, sometimes defending, sometimes admitting, but the discussion was at best very desultory and the group was growing bored and impatient. The Press was suggested, and it seemed that Ginny would be a good adversary because, for some unclear reasons, their difficulties seemed related.

Ginny got up, and to the surprise of all, methodically took off earrings, watch, rings, and shoes, and planted herself solidly, legs apart on the floor. She looked ready for business. Mike took off his shoes, stood up in front of her, reached out, quickly hooked his leg behind her, and began to slam her to the floor wrestler-style. Ginny grappled desperately and the two of them swung around in wild circles until Ginny finally went down. She then squirmed and twisted but finally had to give up under Mike's superior strength. He helped her up with her cooperation. In turn, she was able to get him down with only moderate resistance and he helped her get him up.

Following are the accounts of the incident given by Mike and Ginny.

Mike's account: I really don't remember how far into the two-week lab this event occurred, but somehow I feel it was in the evening session. Ginny had, for me, assumed a particular significance within the group. There was some feeling of sexual desire on my part for her, and at the same time she assumed some kind of mother role. She and Roberto were very close at that time. I felt myself competing with him for Ginny's attention. Ginny had been responding to me in a way that was accepting and also playful. There were many invitations across the open space of the group from Ginny to me when she felt she wanted to dance, but there was also very little contact with Ginny outside of the group meetings.

The event preceding the press between Ginny and me that had the most impact on me, at the feeling level, was the press between Shelly and Herb. My memory of this is that the press between Shelly and Herb occurred in the afternoon, right after lunch, and the feelings that I had about Shelly were that he looked like a fat little kid trying to press very ineffectually down on Herb. I got angry at him, and when Shelly then said in effect to Herb, "Won't you please lay down?" and Herb complied, my anger was mixed with disgust for Shelly.

In the next session, we were discussing the press between Shelly and Herb and either Ginny

said she would like to try it and I volunteered or
. . . I said I would like to try it and Ginny volunteered. The latter seems more accurate because
I remember that I was standing in the middle of
the group alone, without anyone in front of me,
and I was feeling scared because I didn't know
whether anyone stronger than myself was going
to come into the center. I experienced a real flash
of fear when I thought that Frank [a three-hun-
dred-pound black-belt judo expert] might come in,
because at that point my feelings were that I
didn't care who was going to come into the center
so much as whoever came would have to go down.
The part I have just described is still very clear
in my mind and I can still see myself standing,
looking over Herb's head and out of the window
of the room that we were in. I had my feet spread
apart and in my old "gang fight" stance, with my
chest puffed out and trying like hell not to let on
that I was scared stiff.

Ginny came into the center and faced me, we
put our hands on each other's shoulders, but before any action took place I remember saying to
Ginny, "I want you to fight back," and she replied,
"Don't worry, I will." Right after that I began
to press down on Ginny's shoulders and tried to
get her a little off-balance; she resisted, and resisted quite firmly, and responded to my press
with an awful lot of strength, a surprising amount
of strength. My next reaction was one of complete
fear, and so I cocked my foot behind her legs
and threw her over my hip. As she went down
I tried to get my knee on her back. Ginny was (in
terms of her later report) thoroughly enjoying this,
and was resisting by trying to crawl away. My re-

action to all this was rather frightening. I was consciously going after her large bones—the shoulders and leg muscle area—to try and get a good grip on her and try to hold her down, without her being able to get away and without hurting her. Yet as each second went by and she was successfully getting away from me, it seemed that a voice in my head was yelling at her, "Stay down, damn you; stay down!" Ginny was flat on the floor on her stomach and wriggling away from me. I had one hand on her shoulder and the other on her thigh and was trying to get my knee across her back to pin her down with my weight so she couldn't get away. If that wasn't too successful I was going to go after her wrist and bend her arm up behind her back but she was *going to stay down!*

I finally succeeded and pinned Ginny so that she gave up. Ginny and I stayed in that position for just a few seconds and I remember that at one point it was, for me, no longer Ginny there, and I got up and walked away as if she were a bundle of clothes lying on the floor. It took the rest of the group to call my attention to the fact that I had to go back and help Ginny up as part of the agreement of the press. I turned around and did so, without any feelings toward Ginny but with a great feeling of elation within myself. I didn't feel any pride in having put Ginny down, but I really felt very good that I *had* put Ginny down. Part of the experience is the comments that came from the group members, Frank saying, "I wanted to kick you in the balls." Herb looked at me and said that it had been the most disgusting display he had ever seen, and Shelly's comment was "You just threw my mother down, and I don't know if I like it." I remember you asking me if I would do it again if I had to do it again, and my response was that it wasn't necessary for me to do it again but if Ginny and I did press again I felt that I would press her all the way to the floor again only because of the reactions of the males in the group. My exact comment was, "I think it would do the group good." I also remember at this point that none of the women reacted in the same way that the men did, they seemed to envy or enjoy Ginny whose report was exhilaration and a very, very good feeling at having rough-housed with a man.

Ginny never realized or experienced any fear throughout the press, and yet I was very much aware of my own feeling state. I was willing and ready to hurt in order to keep her down. The two things that I am quite clear about, although I don't know exactly how they occurred, were: I felt good, real good, and, second, a remark that I made, either in the group that night, or sometime later, was that "I threw an awful lot of women down when I threw Ginny down." Some of these were my mother, my older sister, a female team-member of mine that I had come to the workshop with. The best description of what happened is that I experienced myself and my masculinity in a way in which I had never before had the opportunity.

The most immediate effect that I remember this event had upon me was a feeling of release. Up until then, most of my relationships with females were in the form of a double-bind. It took the form of sexual-arousal but not so much an arousal out of desire as a feeling of the need to completely dominate and make subservient to my needs, through sexual intercourse, any woman I had a relationship with, business or social. The other end of the bind was a very strong feeling of sexual inadequacy on my part, so that in my fantasy, my dreams of conquest were always tinged with the fear of failure. The most important thing that happened to that double-bind because of the press was not that it disappeared, but that it no longer had the same debilitating effect on me. It now allowed me to engage in a more reality-oriented relationship with women. I could begin to confront a woman who had been placed—either by virtue or authority or responsibility—in a position that was superior to mine, in a way that was, to me, healthy, in that I expressed myself and my feelings, strong as well as weak. It opened up an area of tenderness in my relationships at home with my wife and children, a feeling that I had always been hiding for fear that it was weakness. In fact, it is in the area of home relationships that I feel I have gained the most. I guess the phrase "A lot of women in my life went down when Ginny went down" is most appropriate and descriptive.

Ginny's account: The encounter with Mike, at the time, seemed to me fun and exciting but not especially important or unusual. I was at first astonished by the big reaction of other members of the group, including our trainer, and how much more important it seemed to Mike and to them than it had seemed to me. However, in retrospect I have used it to sort out some of my attitudes toward men—unlike many therapeutic experiences, all on the positive side. I think the encounter with Mike helped me understand and integrate some of the positive aspects of my relationships with men, especially my relationships with men as a strong woman deeply involved in her profession.

Mike to me was a handsome, virile, young guy, enough younger than myself so that there could be no question of a real flirtation, attractive enough so that I had enjoyed playing tennis with him the day before. He didn't know the rules of tennis at all, not even how to score. I'm not a good tennis player, but I've played a lot, and so it seemed natural to me to tell him about how the game is played and scored, especially since he said he wanted to know. I was astonished when the next day or so in the T-group, it turned out that he had deeply resented my taking what to him seemed a leadership attitude, and that this had led to his identifying me with an older woman in the same profession as mine, whose domination he had gotten very much hung-up on.

Our trainer, leading up to it in a way which was natural enough for me not to notice how he did it, suggested that we try to wrestle one another to a fall. I was gleeful. I always enjoy physical activity and had been tired of sitting still. I also enjoy physical contact with people in general. I immediately took off my wristwatch and my rings, including a ring with a very prominent stone which I always wear (this proved important later). Much later, days later, someone in the group said, "I never saw a woman strip so fast." I suppose there was a nicely sublimated sexual element in this.

So I found myself face to face with Mike. He

said, very seriously, "Will you really?" I was amazed that he asked the question. I always try as hard as I can at anything I do, or else it bores me and I won't do it at all. It never entered my mind that I might get hurt. I knew perfectly well that an athletic young man could easily get down a semiathletic, middle-aged woman, without hurting her one bit. I saw myself at some level as wrestling with a boy friend on the sand at Jones Beach. I expected to wrestle as hard as I could and that Mike would put me down without hurting me.

This happened. I was amused and delighted by the ease with which he got me down, and by the fun it was to struggle. I began to laugh.

I don't remember the interval between that and the reaction of the group, but I do remember their reaction. Two members, both as it happened—by chance or not by chance?—very heavy, strong, successful, conventional businessmen, it turned out, had been utterly appalled. They had seen a man strong-arming and perhaps damaging a woman. They had been about to intervene. I thought this was ridiculous. It never occurred to me not to trust Mike or my trainer. (Perhaps, since you want all my thoughts, I should add that I would not have trusted, and did not trust, either Mike or my trainer on an emotional or psychological level. That is, I would not have placed myself in either of their hands psychologically as I did physically. But I do believe that it never occurred to me that I could get hurt, physically.)

My next surprise, a few days later, was to find (as I recall it, and of course I know that memory can make absurd distortions even at the time—

and even more so a year-and-a-half later—), that my trainer felt that he had taken much too big a chance; that he had not expected either Mike or me to carry it through; and that he was frightened when he saw us really fighting. I was rather pleased with myself. "Oh, you didn't know how much trust and courage I had? Well, you found out." [Ginny is quite right. This is the first time I had ever tried this in a group. I feel secure about it now.]

I think quite seriously that what the trainer did not know consciously, but probably knew on some level, is that both Mike and I were physical people, used to sports and physical contacts, and that everybody really knew that he could and would get me down without hurting me, and also that I would not resist in any way which could or would arouse his sadism—in which case, the whole situation would of course have become dangerous for several people—for Mike psychologically, for myself physically, for a number of people if Frankie or Shelly had jumped into the fray, for the trainer if it had been a mess, etc., etc.

Mike's attitude toward me changed sharply after that. He began to enjoy me and admire me as a woman. I was in need of admiration, and was nourished by this. He lit my cigarettes, held my coat, danced with me, and in general treated me as an attractive woman. He never made other than a pleasant conventional verbal pass at me and never attempted to see me afterwards, nor would I have been interested if he had done so.

Now, what did I get out of this? In retrospect, quite a lot. I have been moving through the years toward an increased acceptance and enjoyment of my body after a childhood as a semi-immobilized invalid, and this is one of a long series of episodes that has contributed to my progress. I also recall now very clearly, although at the time it meant nothing to me, that I took off a ring which is sufficiently large and sharp so that it could be a dangerous weapon. I did not even think of why I took it off, but I think now that if my ring had been left on, and had scratched Mike accidentally, the whole situation could have become extremely ugly and even perhaps dangerous. I think that there was something in me basically nice and decent that made me take off my ring.

Also, although again this is only one episode among many, I think I recognized how much I enjoy trusting the strength of a man. In recent years I have become conscious of something about myself which I like very much—that I can teach and supervise men who in some cases are of my own generation, without making them feel that they are castrated by a woman. I see this usually as a kind of intuitive recognition on their part that I am not competing by my achievements, but am trying to please (my father loved me when I got all A's on my report card, and he was a very masculine, strong man). Nonetheless, in our culture it often feels awkward and embarrassing to be a strong and successful woman, especially if one's movements are naturally quick and one's voice naturally carries. I refuse to pose as weak and submissive, and I somehow always fear and expect more disapproval than I usually get for being adequate.

So, it was a lot of fun to be put down by Mike. I trusted Mike to get me down without hurting me.

I trusted my trainer to know what he was doing. On some level which at the time was invisible to me, I trusted myself to take off my potentially scratchy ring. And it was a very nice experience.

What happened: The complementary nature of the interaction helps explain its success. Mike needed to confront his unconfrontable women, and Ginny needed to feel a man's strength to support her feelings of femininity. Ginny's analytic account (she is a psychologist) covers the major points of a technical nature as well as personal.

The apparent physical danger of this activity is, so far, more apparent than real. I have never seen any physical damage beyond scratches in the many presses observed. Proper cautions are required but, as both Ginny and Mike indicated, people don't usually want to actually hurt each other in a situation like this.

The next method is similar, and the example is a good illustration of the value of combining several techniques to achieve an end.

PUSHING

When: Pushing is a useful method in competitive situations where the feelings between the two people are not clear, or when feelings between leader and member are unclear, or when it is desirable to increase involvement.

How: The two participants stand facing each other and clasp both hands, palm to palm, intertwining fingers. When they agree, they begin pushing each other, attempting to make the other give ground. They stop whenever they want to.

Cautions: This requires exertion and space. Persons whose physical condition precludes exertion should be excluded. The physical space should be large enough and not contain exposed breakable, sharp, pointed, or dangerous objects, especially radiators.

Example: Roger was having a great deal of difficulty with the leader. At the beginning of the meetings he took an extremely subservient role, asking such questions as, "Do I have to answer any question you ask me?" To bring him to a peer relation with the leader became one objective of the group. One member suggested that he push with the leader to try to help achieve this aim. He refused. He was unable to relate comfortably to the leader until the following sequence. A group fantasy had revealed his tendencies toward self-blame. This uncovering led to a discussion of the pain he had suffered as an unwanted child with attendant feelings of insignificance and worthlessness. He then was put into an individual fantasy during which the childhood situation was worked on. The fantasy involved crying and much anguish, finally resulting in an acceptance of his childhood status. Immediately upon finishing the fantasy he leaped up and said he wanted to push with the leader. We spent about five minutes pushing each other around the room, ending with a spontaneous, warm embrace. Our relation thereafter was indeed one between equals. He even began to challenge several of my suggestions and generally behaved very appropriately. This behavior continued without backsliding.

What happened: The first suggestion for the push was premature. It was too mechanical, being a "gimmick" at that point since, although appropriate to the situation, it did not have sufficient support from the previous relationship to be meaningful. The characteristic that prevented the group member from relating realistically to the leader was tied to his feelings of self-worth which, in turn, went back to his childhood. Dealing with this feeling with the aid of fantasy helped to strengthen his self-concept to the extent that he was able to confront the leader. The opportunity to immediately test his new self-image with the leader by a method that allowed the emotions to be felt throughout the whole body solidified his feeling of self-worth and helped him work out one consequence of the inadequate self-concept, namely an excessive subservient attitude toward leaders.

The following method is aimed at relieving excessive internal control rather than external. It uses the group to externalize what is happening within a person.

BREAKING OUT

When: Breaking out is usually a very valuable exercise for constricted people needing to break through inhibitions, people who feel immobilized, unable to move, or to do what they would like to do.

How: The group forms a tight circle, interlocking arms. If the group is very large, members form two concentric circles. One person stands in the middle of the inner circle and must break out in any way he can, over, under, or bursting through. Members of the circle try their utmost to contain him and not let him out.

The method can be extended to a situation where a person feels constricted by one other individual, as in the case of a person feeling tied down by his spouse. In this case, the constrictor stands in back of the person he is presumably constricting and wraps his arms around the arms of the other, pinning the constrictee's arms tightly. The constrictee then tries to break out.

Cautions: This experience is often very strenuous. Anyone with a heart condition or any physical condition where vigorous activities is unwise should not participate. Also, since the circle may move about, it is wise to have ample room and no obstacles that may break or harm a participant.

Example: Nancy, a twenty-four-year-old girl, was trying to deal with her problem of being too tight and constricted. She spoke in a low and controlled voice, and was always very logical and organized. Her face was usually expressionless, her movements were stiff and graceless, and her relations with people lacked spontaneity and vitality. She had had an earlier fantasy in which she entered her body and found her father fastening down all the organs of her body with steel straps. This, together with her recollection of early childhood, pointed to the central role of her father in her constriction. These considerations led to a psychodrama in which she confronted her father, portrayed by another group member. Here she tried to express to him the feelings that she had never been able to articulate to him directly. When she attempted to declare her independence of him she weakened, her voice faltered, and she reverted to infantile behavior. At this point something was required to give her the additional strength and confidence necessary for her psychodramatic confrontation with her father. She was transferred from the psychodrama to the breaking-out situation. Her frustration led her to start out furiously, pounding fiercely at the people in the circle, but the group held fast and she fell to the floor exhausted and, characteristically, gave up. But the group wouldn't let her. They simply reminded her that she hadn't yet broken out, and they stood their ground around her. This unexpected reaction sparked her to get up and try again. Following a lengthy and combative exchange, she finally smashed through.

After catching her breath she was asked to return to the psychodrama. Immediately on her return she grabbed the group member enacting her father, put him down, placed her knee on his chest, and told him that he was never going to hold her back again, in a very articulate and forceful statement.

She felt elated directly after the experience and her behavior changed markedly thereafter. She was lighter and gayer, became much more feminine, her face brightened, and her relations became more informal.

What happened: The experience of physically overcoming a constricting force was a new one for this girl. Feeling the experience in every muscle of the body gave her confidence. She discovered that she was capable of such behavior. Immediately relating it to the source of the original constriction, her father, allowed her to restructure the original situation in such a way that it was now within her capabilities to deal with. The total physical involvement made the experience more meaningful and lasting.

A key point in the experience came when the group would not let Nancy out after her first attempt at breaking through. Her behavior was typical of her life—to make one try, and then give up. She was now startled to find that this behavior wouldn't work. She had to find some new way of dealing with the situation. Her ability to come through at this point, *to try though her arms were too weary,* led to her revised view of her capacities and the feeling of exhilaration. That this was a lasting change is reflected in the following comments she made upon reading this account of the event.

Nancy's comments: A few thoughts on my case.

It seems accurate and seems to capture the essence of what happened. When I was giving up I can remember being reminded that I wasn't out. I can also remember someone kicking me.

Returning to the psychodrama after breaking out is very dim in my mind, interestingly enough . . .

Right after the breaking out I can remember feeling more alive, excited and *greater* than I ever have in my life. It was extremely significant. There was a feeling of release that I never would have dreamed possible. The *joy* was unbelievable.

I've felt different ever since. The weekend that followed I talked incessantly to a friend who had just returned from Japan, and we explored some issues that we'd never dared to explore before.

Now, two months later, many of the feelings and changes still remain. Last week, someone commented that I looked like I'd gone through a metamorphosis and that it appeared to be more than superficial. Several other people have commented that I seem and look different. Several people said that I look sexier.

I've felt more feminine, more open, more spontaneous. I've done new things . . . painted the bathroom apricot, worked in painting, gone on a diet that I stuck to for once, changed some of my clothes style, joined an exercise class, sought a modern-dance class. I've enjoyed the present more, exposed more of myself. I've made a couple of major decisions . . . like to become a full-time student next year and complete my doctor's degree. In general I've been less pressured internally and more available to my feelings. I've spent more time with people I enjoy. I've done more things that I want to do. I've spent more money. (Father is very Scotch.)

I've been somewhat less fearful of being judged by others . . . and more open with authorities. I've been less fearful of being me, strong, angry, etc. I've said no to things when previously I might have hesitated.

It often amazes me that many of the positive things I have felt have stayed with me. Sometimes it scares me that they won't.

The non-verbal techniques, again based on the conversion of feeling into a physical equivalent, are especially effective in the control area. People so seldom mobilize their full energies and test their strength that the sense of aliveness resulting from the exertion is itself a very stimulating experience. Beyond that, the feelings about control are usually very closely tied, at bottom, to physical fears and concerns so that non-verbal methods are particularly suitable.

These methods help to clarify feelings of power, competition, strength, and effectiveness, and provide situations where the use of a more than usual amount of competence and strength is required from an individual. The effective use of his own resources allows a person to develop his coping ability and increase his feelings of competence and potency. He is given an opportunity to try things that formerly seemed beyond his ability. Being able "to fight the unbeatable foe," or the foe that once seemed unbeatable, allows him to view his own capacities anew, and often a strengthening of his concept of himself follows. Exhilaration and a renewed surge of energy is the immediate result.

Usually following resolution of the control issues, feelings of affection begin to emerge. To clarify and develop these feelings and make them a further source of joy in the relations between people, more tender approaches are required.

Affection

Since affection is based on the building of emotional ties, it is usually the last phase to emerge in the development of a human relation, following inclusion and control. In the inclusion phase, people must *encounter* each other and decide to continue their relation; control issues require them to *confront* one another and work out how they will be related; then, to continue the relation, affection ties must form and people must *embrace* each other to form a lasting bond.

The person with too little affection, the under-personal, tends to avoid close, personal ties with others. He maintains his two-person relations on a superficial, distant level and is most comfortable when others do the same with him. Consciously, he wishes to maintain this emotional distance, and frequently expresses a desire not to get "emotionally involved," while unconsciously he seeks a satisfactory affectional relation. His fear is that no one loves him. In a group situation he is afraid he won't be liked. He has great difficulty genuinely liking people, and distrusts their feelings toward him.

His attitude could be summarized by this statement, "I find the affection area very painful since I have been rejected; therefore, I shall avoid close personal relations in the future." The "direct technique" for maintaining emotional distance is to reject and avoid people in order to actively prevent emotional closeness or involvement, even to the point of being antagonistic. The "subtle technique" is to be superficially friendly to everyone. This behavior acts as a safeguard against having to get close to, or become personal with, any *one* person.

The deepest anxiety for the underpersonal, that regarding the self, is that he is unlovable. If people got to know him well, he believes, they would discover the traits that make him so unlovable. As opposed to the inclusion anxiety that the self is of no value, worthless, and empty, and the control anxiety that the self is stupid and irresponsible, the affection anxiety is that the self is nasty and unlovable.

The overpersonal type attempts to become extremely close to others. He definitely wants others to treat him in a very close, personal way. The unconscious feeling on which he is operating is, "My first experiences with affection were painful, but perhaps if I try again they will turn out to be better." Being liked is extremely important to him in his attempt to relieve his anxiety about being always rejected and unlovable. The direct technique for being liked is an overt attempt to gain approval, be extremely personal, ingratiating, intimate, and confiding. The subtle technique is more manipulative, to devour friends and subtly punish any attempts by them to establish other friendships, and to be possessive.

The underlying feelings are the same as those for the underpersonal. Both the overpersonal and the underpersonal responses are extreme, both are motivated by a strong need for affection, both are accompanied by strong anxiety about ever being loved (and basically about being unlovable), and both have considerable hostility behind them stemming from the anticipation of rejection.

For the individual who successfully resolved his affectional relations with others in childhood, close emotional relations with one other person present no problem. He is comfortable in such a personal relation, and he can also relate comfortably in a situation requiring emotional distance. It is important for him to be liked, but if he isn't liked he can accept the fact that the dislike is the result of the relation between himself and one other person

—in other words, the dislike does not mean that he is an unlovable person. Unconsciously, he feels that he is a lovable person who is lovable even to people who know him well. And he is capable of giving genuine affection.

The primary interaction of the affection area is that of *embrace,* either literal or symbolic. The expression of appropriate deeper feelings is the major issue. In most groups a paradox arises around this issue. At the beginning of the group there are many expressions as to how difficult it is to express hostility to people. It often later develops that there is only one thing more difficult—expressing warm, positive feelings.

Affectional problems, both giving and taking, are usually very profound. There are affectional elements in many of the foregoing techniques, especially the encounter and the two-person group fantasy. The following method, however, focuses directly on affectional problems.

GIVE AND TAKE AFFECTION

When: For most people giving affection and receiving affection are very difficult matters. Many people feel that they are unlovable and that any gestures of affection or liking or admiration are extremely hard for them to accept. If a person "knows" he is unlovable, how can he believe it when someone professes love? For these situations there are methods to help the person experience fully the affection felt for him by others. At the same time the others have the opportunity to experience themselves giving, or being reluctant to give, affection.

How: There are two approaches to this situation, verbal and non-verbal. The non-verbal is usually a more powerful experience but for the best results it should be used after the group has developed close feelings.

The verbal method has been called "strength bombardment."[3] The group members are asked to tell the person who is the focus of their attention all the positive feelings they have about him. He is just to listen. The intensity of the experience may be varied in a number of ways. Probably the simplest procedure is to have the focus leave the circle, put his back to the group and overhear what is said. Or he can be kept in the group and talked to directly. A stronger impact occurs when each person stands in front of the focus, touches him, looks him in the eye, and tells him directly.

The non-verbal give-and-take requires the focus to stand in the center of a circle made up of the other members of the group. He is to shut his eyes and the other members are all to approach him and express their positive feelings non-verbally in whatever way they wish. This usually takes the form of hugging, stroking, massaging, lifting, or whatever each person feels. If the situation is timely this procedure almost always develops into tears both for the focus and for some group members. The experience of massive affection is a very unusual one, and the feelings in the participants about expressing affection usually vary widely. For some who can't feel affection to the same degree as the others, this exercise is very disturbing and

---

[3] This method has been written about by Herbert Otto. A similar technique is used in psychodrama.

offers a valuable insight to be developed further. The exercise is concluded by a mutual feeling that it is over. Sometimes discussion is useful, but more often the feelings are so strong that talking dilutes them, and the group prefers not to talk.

Caution: There are no special cautions to be taken other than to anticipate that the effect may be powerful and that crying is not uncommon.

Examples: Suzy, a Chinese girl of seventeen, was a member of a mixed group of adults and teenagers. The group was a cross-section of the school community, consisting of parents, teachers, the superintendent, and several eleventh graders (see Intergenerational, page 215). Suzy felt oppressed by her strict, old-country upbringing and her own inadequate self-concept to such an extent that she was totally incapable of trusting any remark of a positive nature made to her. However, if there were a hint of anything non-positive she would hear it clearly, believe it, exaggerate it, and use it to confirm her own picture of herself. Words couldn't help, although she actually engendered very warm feelings from virtually the whole group. The give-and-take-affection exercise was suggested and she immediately began to cry as the first few people made contact with her. She broke down completely in the arms of one of the male teachers. Crying was very unusual for Suzy. Her "cool" exterior had prevented anything from bringing her to tears for years. The whole experience was so moving that several others began to cry. Suzy could not talk to anyone for an hour or so after. No one spoke, and the group gradually drifted off in pairs and trios to take walks and talk quietly.

Following is Suzy's charming and pithy description of the event.

Suzy's account: A sixteen-year-old had narrow steps outside her front door which headed in one direction, and the intersections I approached could not open into new streets. For long ago, it was decided which turns I was to take, where I was to bear right and where I was not to bear left. I was told where to attend school in the future, and my interests were chosen for me. I felt like a small child dragged by the arm across the streets.

I had just finished telling my sad tale during the T-group session, when I was placed in the center of the room. An interchange of physical feelings were shown. For the first time in a long time, I started to sniffle, and when I reached my history teacher I was sobbing uncontrollably. I felt that I actually meant something to my teacher and to the others rather than a funny diversion who was fun to have around. And, for the moment, I was sharing something of significance with someone else. After this session my brain could not quite function and I could not perceive what tangible change it had left me with. When I returned to school the next day, a period of constant high ecstasy followed. Starting with that day in school, I saw and accepted what others meant to me and what I had meant to others.

What happened: Words had helped Suzy maintain her distance. When she spoke she looked away and kept the human contact to a minimum, so that words were not a channel through which she could be reached. The non-verbal behavior penetrated her defenses and contacted feelings of sadness and longing from which she had cut herself off. The special significance of the male teacher underlined the important role of her father in her sense of deprivation of affection and consequent feelings of being unlovable. The experiencing of her strong need for affection helped to readjust her. She began to turn away from the inability to feel affection—actually a massive escape from her longing—and now looked toward the problem itself. She could better face the difficulties in the parental situation and work toward a resolution of those feelings with a possible increase in self-esteem. It had been extremely difficult, if not impossible, to reach her without using a non-verbal method of great intensity to put her in contact with her real feelings. In Suzy's situation, her self-esteem was so low that this experience, effective as it was, would have to be followed up soon or else the effect would fade.

Important insight can occur to the affection giver as well as the receiver during these give-and-take sessions. The experience of being in the center was offered to every member of the group. At the completion everyone discussed his reaction. One woman reported a discovery as a giver of affection that later turned out to be one of her key experiences in the workshop. She said that about halfway through the exercise she realized that she was trying to figure out what each person wanted and then give it to them. At one point it struck her that she wasn't even considering what *she* wanted to give. From then on she started giving them what she wanted to give them and to her surprise she found that in almost every case they enjoyed and appreciated what she wanted to give. The very fact that she wanted to give it, she reported, made it more valuable and desirable to the recipient.

This allowed her to understand better some difficulties she had in her work life where people tended not to treat her as a sufficiently significant individual. She not only wasn't giving to people in the way she wanted to, but she didn't even let herself acknowledge how she felt about it. She was too busy trying to gratify others regardless of her own wishes. As she lived with this new idea, the realization overtook her that she could also go too far in the other direction by only considering what she wanted to give. Real giving involves a combination of what someone wants and needs to get, and what the other one wants and needs to give. But she was well on the way to opening up an important new area in her relations with people, precipitated by the feelings she had experienced in trying to give non-verbally.

The next activity involves giving pleasure to someone, a vital ingredient of the affection area.

ROLL AND ROCK

When: One of the central issues of affection is trusting the feelings of others. The other side of this trust is the ability to gratify and give pleasure to someone who trusts. When it is important to demonstrate or test trust, or to find a mode of giving pleasure to someone, the roll and rock is an excellent device.

How: The person in need of trust-testing stands in the center of the group, with all other members forming a circle around him. The group is asked to pass him around the circle from person to person. He is to close his eyes, try to relax every muscle in his body, and try to give himself over to the other group members. The group members then pass him around the circle several times. Often he is stiff and controlled at the beginning, but begins to relax as the circuits increase. Then the others pick him up and hold him at chest level parallel to the floor, supporting all muscles. It is usually best to have his hands and arms rest on his chest and stomach, and let his head fall back naturally just holding two fingers under it to take away the tension on his neck. Then he is gently swayed back and forth, the group members being careful to make as little noise as possible. Continuing the swaying motion, the group begins to lower him until he is placed gently on the floor. All hands are removed from the body slowly and tenderly.

A possible addition is to pause briefly after the lowering, and then stretch him so that his muscle tensions are reduced. His arms are placed gently straight over his head. Someone grasps his wrists. Another person grasps his ankles, and another puts one hand under the chin and the other under the back of the skull. A fourth person crouches over the stomach to direct the activity. The director places his hands together to indicate the starting point before the stretching begins. He then slowly moves his hands apart to coordinate the pull of the three stretchers. Each of them pulls away from the center of the body with a slow, firm pull. The pull can be extremely strong without injury or pain, and the stronger the pull usually the more pleasure for the stretchee. The director parts his hands widely until the maximum stretch is obtained. Then slowly the director's hands come back together, the stretchers gradually relax their pull, and slowly their hands glide away from the body. The stretched one is left on the ground until he chooses to rise.

A two-person variation of this method may be used to test the trust of one person for another. In this technique one person turns his back on another and lets himself fall backwards and be caught by the other. The feelings of trust or distrust are usually felt very clearly in this situation. *Caution:* Although a great deal of physical activity is required, there seems to be little risk involved. There should be a sufficient number of people with enough cumulative strength to be able to support the person in the center. In the stretch, the stretchee should immediately notify the stretchers if he feels any discomfort.

Example: Evelyn was having a great deal of trouble getting into the group. She was able to empathize a great deal with other people, but had great difficulty expressing feelings about herself. When attention focused on her it became clear that one of her central problems was trust. She didn't trust the group. To make this feeling sharper she was asked to fall backwards and rely on the leader—the one whom she said she distrusted least—to catch her. This was virtually impossible for her to do. After further exploration she was asked to try the roll and rock, to again experience her feelings about trust with the group and also perhaps to go further into her difficulty. Following is Evelyn's description of her experience.

Evelyn's account: Then the group surrounded me in a tight circle, and I was told to roll against them. With a feeling of relief I fell backwards into the bodies, some firm, some soft, as I was propelled around the alternating men and women making up the amazingly secure enclosure which did not seem to yield in any way against my weight. Someone told me to relax my knees, so I collapsed them to find that I was already totally supported by the members who easily and almost weightlessly passed me from one to another. There was no sense of self—just of movement and strong hands supporting me as I was passed around and around. I felt blissful, as though it could go on forever.

A far-away voice said, "Pick her up," and the whole group, as though they were one, lifted me gently in the air. Cradling me in their arms, they began rocking me backwards and forwards. The swinging produced a sensation in my stomach like that when a roller coaster takes its first plunge. I felt somehow that I was being swung from one end of the room to the other, and was surprised later when we rocked someone else that the movement was so gentle. One of my hands with fingers spread lightly covered my face; the other was held by a member of the group. Tears flowed out of the sides of my eyes. I felt in complete ecstasy—totally beyond myself.

I became conscious that I was sighing rhythmically in response to each swing, and that these reactions were remarkably similar to those of the sexual act. With this realization the rapture began to subside. No embarrassment accompanied the thought, but it did seem to me that in some way the rhythmical sensations in my stomach and the cries were representative of the state. The previous exercises must have built up feelings of trust and the fantasy of the cave must have broken down psychic barriers making this possible. It had been brought on in the arms of the world, and I felt that the enactment of that ritual could exonerate me from the pressures of long accumulated guilt.

They placed me gently on the floor, and I was eager to arise and return to my chair, for the experience seemed complete, and in some way, I knew that what I had come to the workshop for, had happened. Still on the floor, I was asked, "What do you want to do now?" and I affirmatively answered, "Go home."

Feeling exhilarated, I began to try to answer the questions of the group who seemed to know that something important had happened to me, but did not know what. I said it was like having a baby, because in both instances in states of semi-consciousness a hand had clasped mine and supported me meaningfully throughout. They also wondered why I had become so calm so soon afterward, but the combined feelings of release and rapture after both making love and giving birth seemed identical to the feelings I had then. Other questions they asked reassured me that no one had understood what had happened, so I saved face, at the same time having exposed myself symbolically in a way I most feared in all of life.

The day after the meeting I felt overwhelmingly in love but there was no one to whom I could apply the emotion.

What seems important to me about this experience is not the emotional representation of the sexual act, but the occurrence of it (symbolically) before a group. Since childhood I have always experienced a group as hostile, in the sense of pointing fingers at me in sexual accusations. I have never been able to overcome this fright. Perhaps, having undergone emotionally the very exposure I feared the most, and finding support and trust from the group instead of a whipping, I might be able to overcome this terror.

What happened: As with the other non-verbal techniques, the feeling engendered by the actual physical support seems to exceed the feeling that comes through the verbal representation. When a person actually surrenders his whole body to others and finds that they will take care of him, he must examine his feelings toward them in a new way. The experience of giving to a person through these physical means also usually proves very rewarding. It is a more direct, complete expression than the verbalization. Cooperating with others in the circle brings about a feeling of togetherness in the common task of giving pleasure to another.

In Evelyn's case the movement immediately connected to two very meaningful experiences in her life, childbirth and intercourse, and rather quickly led her into the area probably at the basis of her distrust of groups—her fear that they are "pointing fingers at me in sexual accusations," and that they would whip her. The group was able to help her "to right the unrightable wrong," her early sexual thoughts. The combination of the intellectual realization, and having a new experience in which she was supported and trusted by the group instead of whipped, seems to have helped her make great strides toward overcoming her fear and distrust of people and allowing her to express herself more fully. The feeling of overwhelming love that came after the experience is another instance of joy following release and a new availability of more potential for feeling and expression.

The methods used to develop the potential for affection rely heavily on the close tie between physical touch and affectionate feelings. Both the *roll and rock* and *give and take affection* center around the human caress as the way to bring out and clarify feelings of wanting affection and giving affection. They also provide an opportunity to try out affectionate gestures that have often been suppressed for many years, and to allow an individual to experience his potential for giving and receiving love. Successful experiences can greatly restructure a person's self-concept in the direction of helping him feel more loving and lovable.

The interpersonal-relations methods aid in the process of encounter, confrontation, and embrace between people. Successful experiences enrich man's capacity for enjoying other people through enhancing his feelings about himself in relation to them.

Unfortunately, cultural and organizational forces

are often powerful deterrents to joyful feelings. Combinations of techniques and more complex approaches must be devised to meet these problems.

5 · Organizational Relations

It is essential for our fully realized man to have a well-balanced and fully functioning body, to develop his creative abilities and personal functioning, and to learn to experience rich satisfying relations with others. But he lives in a cultural context. He lives within a family, he works, he belongs to certain racial and religious groups, he is a member of a particular generation, and he functions within a political structure. Each of these memberships can inhibit or facilitate the human potential.

The past few decades have seen an upsurge of interest in using such organizational contexts for the greater development of individual personalities. Methods of handling conflict and encouraging understanding are being used and evolved in many contexts.[1]

These innovations have come primarily through the application of the behavioral sciences to various organizations and social institutions.

---

[1] A good source for further information about organizational relations, and one drawn upon generously in the present account, is E. Schein and W. Bennis, *Personal and Organizational Change through Group Methods,* New York, Wiley, 1965.

Generally these "interventions," as they are usually called, are of three types.

Encounter-group (T-group) training programs. Activities occurring in some groups of this type have been described many times above. A brief word of background is relevant for discussing the use of these groups in organizational context. The idea of "laboratory training," that is, human-relations training at a residential site removed from everyday activities, originated at Bethel, Maine, in 1947, under the auspices of the National Training Laboratories of the National Education Association. The T-group emerged as one of the most important components of laboratory training and has evolved over the past twenty years into a major instrument of organizational change.

The T-group unfolds in an unstructured group setting where the participants examine their interpersonal relationships. In addition to having the characteristics described above for the encounter group, the T-group often includes attempts to understand the dynamics of group norms, roles, communication distortions, and the effects of authority on a number of behavioral patterns, personality and coping mechanisms, etc. The participants learn to analyze and become more sensitive to the processes of human interaction, and acquire concepts to order and control these phenomena.

T-groups are used in organizations today in several ways. In some laboratories, often called "stranger labs," executives attend as "delegates" representing their organizations. The parent organization hopes to improve itself this way by "seeding" a sufficient number of managers.

"Cousin labs" consist of individuals with similar organizational ranks but from different functional groups, e.g., all first-line supervisors or all general foremen. Sometimes T-groups are composed of members of the same company but of different ranks and from different departments. No man is in the same group with anyone from his own work group.

Another popular arrangement is the functional group which is identical to the intact group as it functions in the formal organization: e.g., a particular supervisor and his work group, or a school principal with his teachers.

Consulting. The behavioral science consultant operates very much like a practicing physician or psychotherapist. The consultant starts from the chief presenting symptom of the organization, articulates it in such a way that the causal and underlying mechanisms of the problem are understood, and then takes remedial action.

He employs an extensive repertory of techniques which he uses flexibly, allowing the consultant much latitude. He may interview, observe, administer questionnaires, convene T-groups, encourage confrontation between conflicting elements, teach, create situations which will clarify issues—in short, do whatever his behavioral science training and his ingenuity suggest so as to help his client resolve his difficulties.

Applied Research. Another specific method for attempting to help organizations to function better is for research to be done within the organization and the results used centrally in the consultation.

Survey data are collected and then reported back to the particular departments in "feedback" meetings where the subjects become clients and have a chance to review the findings, test them against their own experiences, and even ask the researchers to test some of their hypotheses. Rather than the traditional uses of research, of a technocratic variety, where the findings are submitted in "triplicate" and probably ignored, this method strives for active participation of the subjects.

In other words, most methods of research application collect information and report it. There the relationship ends. In the survey feedback approach, the collecting and reporting of results is only the beginning of the relationship. On the basis of the research results, and partly because of them, the involvement and participation in the planning, collection, analysis, and interpretation of more data are activated. Providing participants with knowledge of results is the first step of planned change.

These, in quick review, represent the major developments in working with organizations and social systems to increase the atmosphere for developing human potential. There are, of course, other methods as well—family therapy is one— but this is not the place for an extensive review of these methods.

The workings of these methods may be demonstrated by several examples from the author's experience. These are classified by the type of social problem to which the experience was relevant.

Intergenerational and Educational

One of the realities of every historical era is that several generations coexist and inevitably find areas of conflict. Failure to resolve these conflicts may have a far-reaching and damaging effect on attempts to develop human potential beyond the level of the earlier generation.

Two experiences illustrate the various effects of different modes of handling these problems. Several years ago, the student leaders at a large western university asked the author to conduct a "leadership laboratory" for about eighty leaders of various student organizations. These students wanted to learn about how to perform their leadership functions more effectively, how to work better with each other, and how to communicate better with the school administration. For the latter purpose, they invited some twenty to forty of the top administrative officials of the university.

This was a university where the students had great concern over the increasing impersonality of the institution and their lack of contact with the administration. Their invitation was a conscious plea to establish a relation with the administration that would be supportive to their growth as students and as individuals. They wanted to meet with the administration in a retreat several hundred miles from the campus where the atmosphere was informal and feelings could be exchanged.

The workshop was held and was very successful —with one reservation. The attendance of the student leaders was remarkable. Virtually all of the eighty were present. But of all the administrators invited, none appeared. The students' appeal had been totally rebuffed.

Although there were many other important intervening events, it may not be irrelevant that a few months later the campus broke out in a violent student revolt. One of the issues revolved around the feeling of alienation between the students and the administration. Perhaps the attitudes of the latter reflected in the earlier event were among the factors to which the students reacted.

A contrasting approach occurred in a Long Island school district. Here the school administration recognized the strain within the school community and initiated action to deal with it directly. The school-community problems had been accentuated by the recent defeat of a school bond proposal. The community was split along Jewish-Gentile, liberal-conservative, school administration-community lines, and the parents were despairing of the "new generation."

The school superintendent called in behavior-science consultants, including the author, to help him deal with his problems. The joint decision was to set up an encounter group whose members formed a cross-section of the school community. The group would be composed of the school superintendent, four parents—two of whom were active for the school bonds, and Jewish, and two of whom were active against the bonds, and Gentile—three teachers, and seven representative eleventh-grade students chosen by the student body. Here, in one group, it was hoped, all of the salient school-community issues could be explored.

The group was enormously successful from many standpoints. Since it illustrates not only the relations, and the integration of interpersonal problems with work problems (in this case education) this group and the events that followed will be presented in some detail.

The first noticeable difference between students' behavior and adults' behavior in the group was the speed and eagerness with which each wanted to enter into an open and honest exchange of feelings. The students wanted to right away, while the adults felt, "We ought to get to know each other better," "Let's go slow," "We'll have plenty of time," etc. The teenagers finally prevailed, and the group discussed topics such as marijuana, sex, obedience, curfews, respect, loneliness, and competition. From these early sessions, and especially from a retreat in which the whole group spent a weekend meeting away from the school community, a new understanding arose between adults and teenagers. They began to see each other as people, and to break through their mutual stereotypes. Generalization of the experience also occurred as the students began to understand their own parents better and the adults gained new insight into their children.

But valuable as this group was, equally important gain came from the follow-up event. Members of the group decided that one valuable follow-up would be to hold an encounter group for volunteer twelfth graders within their classroom, in order to deal with the emotional and interpersonal problems within a class. Hopefully, this might enhance learning of the class material.

This group was conducted daily for three weeks (fifteen two-to-three hour sessions) in a twelfth-grade social-studies class conducted by a teacher who was a member of the cross-section group. The teacher was a member of the classroom encounter group. The results were complex and often unanticipated.

One outcome of this group is that the children are much more aware of their own needs, wants, and identity. They are much less conformist because they don't need to be. Relations with their parents are, by and large, much renewed. A meeting with the parents was held to inform them of the progress of the group and to hear their reactions.

Following are several reactions from the cross-section group and from the classroom group. They illustrate the range of effects of the project on individuals personally, on the relations among people, on the work of the classroom group, and on the philosophy of education. They describe limitations of the approach, and they present a variety of viewpoints.

The superintendent initiated the project and probably had the greatest investment in its outcome. His reactions are both personal and professional.

Superintendent's reaction: A steering committee of citizens and faculty with a little money to spend thought they ought to spend it to try to find a good way to teach youth who live in a rather homogeneous community how to understand others. We thought to start by working on the age-old understanding gap between youth and adults. I was one of the pilot group of seven fifteen-to-sixteen-year-olds and eight adults. Since I am also the superintendent of the schools which supplied the group's environment and which operates the sequels to our initial program, I have seen the group from three related viewpoints: a delightful personal experience, valuable training and revelation for an administrator, and as an educator who witnessed a potent way of achieving the humanization and individualization of schooling we talk about but seldom do.

The levels are closely related. Had I not experienced the warmth and pleasure of discovering members of my group as friends, I would not have seen the value of the experience to an administrator and to education, nor would I have been in a position to reassure those who would choose to abandon a new experience at the first sign it differed from the old.

My personal experience in our group was one of improved understanding of how I impinge on others and how they impinge on each other; diminished desire to make people over into the image I had for them; and far greater willingness to let my fellows be what they are. I was struck by the willingness of members of the group to go out of their way to heal the hurts of, and offer support to, other members who might have been chastened by some member or members of the group. It was a great pleasure to be liberated from some of the misconceptions and conventions surrounding our relationships, but also a dangerous thing, for outsiders to the group are hardly prepared for openness and frankness; neither do they expect the superintendent of schools to greet a student with a hug after summer vacation. How sad it is that we adults can seldom show spontaneously and physically our friendship.

I was fascinated by the adult-youth interaction. First of all, these were my first youthful friends in years, and, secondly, we adults got a look at our world through youthful eyes without having to tug our grey beards and play the role of wisdom. Yet our experience and view probably illuminated some of what kids thought must be unreal. And, finally, it is exhilarating to begin to feel change in one's feelings towards others and disappointing to know that change is still small.

The possibilities that occur to an administrator as one works in a group with teachers and thinks about typical meetings and encounters seem utopian, and they may be. Think how relaxing it would be to get an honest and open exchange of views, to be able to trust the advice of a colleague who feels like a colleague, not a servitor, or an oppressed one, or a sycophant. How much easier could be the flow of work if we did not load into the process all our hidden meanings and feelings. Two hours spent saying the plan "doesn't make sense just yet" could be cut pretty drastically. But this world doesn't yet lend itself to the administrator's delight. The next group must help the group members deal more effectively with the uninitiated. We've begun offering the group experience to teachers who want it, but as this occurs, other faculty members decide they know what it's all about and draw conclusions from the conversations in the lunch room about what must be going on in the group. They become wary and develop expectations of what the group members should become, which are probably quite unrealistic.

As I see it, then, we all need to be opened up to one another in order to make our organization work better, but we had better be very tolerant of our first attempts to change a lifetime performance in a different mode into a new one.

These remarks emphasize the importance of having the support of the top man before entering an organization. This superintendent's personal experience convinced him of the value of the group and oriented him toward helping the behavioral scientists to work out a most realistic and valuable program. In other situations, if the superintendent is not favorable, the circumstances described could be troublesome enough to cause termination of the project. His reference to the remainder of the faculty underlines the fact that entry into an organization is indeed entering a system of many interdependent parts, all of which must be considered whenever a change is being made in any one. In this case, the classroom group had a considerable impact on teachers and students not in the project, on the principals, and on the parents. Parents' responses will be discussed below.

The superintendent was also very intrigued by the implications of this approach for education. He continues:

I come now to what I think is the most significant thing about our group experience. We think we see the possibility of using this type of experience as a basis for better teaching and learning. We are, in fact, trying this idea out. It's nice to be naive, for if one could anticipate with certainty what lies ahead, he might never set out. That foreboding remark deserves an immediate balance in the statement that I am more convinced than ever that we are on the right track in the attempt to have students deal with their feelings in the class, as well as the content of the subject.

It is difficult yet for me to guess what the best approach would be, but some startling things are already clear. A master teacher—perhaps one of the best anywhere—was never seen by students (before the group experience) as knowing enough about them so that they would ask him to write college recommendations. Neither had he ever before had so many conferences with guidance counselors. To me, this adds up to the conclusion that in our urge to do such a thoughtful job of preparing students in the disciplines we failed to know them and their wants as students.

I think I see the desirablity of having a great many teachers, especially those in the primary grades and in English, social science, and physical education, skilled at leading groups in the discovery of themselves. I now doubt the advisability of turning the classroom into an encounter group. I see great value in a teacher's knowing how to help students reveal themselves as they work in class. I think the intensive group experience is probably best handled for school youth in a camp or similar setting, away from school.

The educational implications of the experience were also very pertinent to the teacher who was a member of the first group and the teacher for the class that had the encounter-group experience.

Teacher's reaction: Somewhere, a long way back, educational jargon, like "meeting individual needs," and "getting along with others," must have been immensely meaningful to the men who coined such phrases. New generations invent new terms to reflect what is meaningful to them. At Hudson, we talk about "transfer." We mean that the only legitimate objective in the teaching of the humanities is that the student shall be changed in such a way as to transcend mere intellectualizing and to become a better, more fulfilled person. I guess we are looking for what you call "joy." We want something to happen to students which inculcates a joy of life they can carry out of the classroom and into life. Pedagogically, we want students to have "meaningful experiences."

Our failures in these attempts have become increasingly evident to me over the years. My experiences over the past year have done much to accelerate this process of disenchantment with even our most progressive methods and objectives. The experiment has clearly demonstrated the futility of all efforts to inculcate or to give students the attitudes we have striven for. We have succeeded only in creating a generation of young people who are surprisingly other-directed. They are unable to distinguish thoughts from feelings— and unable to express feelings even when they recognize them. They are unable to distinguish between their own wants and what their wants "ought to be." Worst of all, many of them feel that love is a kind of dependency which, as a threat to individualism, is a mark of fear.

A year ago I would not have believed it, but it is evident that the cult of "academic excellence" has succeeded to the point where it will be necessary to develop special experiences, like T-groups, in which young people will be encouraged to take the time necessary to discover what it is like to be alive and human.

My state of mind at present makes most progressive methods seem archaic. I am, in theory, converted to the most radical ideas about "self direction" in education. I am, at the same time, convinced that the use of the T-group with older students is a sort of rear-guard action, and that the best hope lies in the training of elementary-school teachers who will use it to best advantage. I wonder where this leaves me? Here I stand, with a career more or less undermined, unwilling to go backward, and not knowing how to go forward.

Again, I am too pessimistic. Although I often feel like the musician who is reaching for a note that can never be played, I am at the same time thrilled with the prospect of new challenges at a point when I might have become bored with it all. None the less, I wish I had sensed more of this twenty years ago.

The need to re-examine old values and challenge shibboleths is part of the quest initiated by the project. It appears that the encounter group provides an experience that is relevant to educational phrases such as "meeting individual needs" and "teaching the whole child," a method that will help to make these phrases more meaningful. The poignant statement about this teacher's undermined career points to a very real issue. This teacher was enormously popular and apparently effective as an "entertainer-teacher." Now he doesn't feel comfortable being that any more and he doesn't know well enough how to integrate his insights from the group experience into his teaching. How can he learn to play his unplayable note? The solution he is finding is to go to the National Training Laboratories Educational Intern program offered in the summer at Bethel, Maine. This will allow him to follow through his group experiences and coordinate them into a new, hopefully more satisfying and effective teaching style. However, the type of upset he feels is a frequent outcome of a successful intervention. It is an almost necessary step prior to rethinking, in terms of joy and meaningfulness, the educational experience.

The viewpoint of the community members in the cross-section group differs from that of school personnel in the focus of interest. Following is a statement from one of the adult members of that group, who is also a parent and a teacher in a neighboring district.

Community member's reaction: I approached our student-adult T-group with considerable hesitation and a good deal of curiosity. The hesitation stemmed from doubt as to whether I really had the time to spend on the project, particularly in view of the fact that I was very hazy indeed on what we would be doing in the group; the curiosity was the product of my interest in teenagers (both as parent and teacher) and of my lack of prior personal relationship with most of the other adults in the group. In short, confusion reigned supreme in my mind, but the whole thing sounded as though it might be fun or instructive, or both.

I can remember some of my feelings during the early sessions of the group rather clearly, although I would be hard put to identify specific incidents. Mostly I was rather uncomfortable—the long silences, the apparent aimlessness of our talk, the lack of structure and definition, all left me feeling odd—somewhat anxious and somewhat bored. I remember talking about the group with friends on several occasions, and commenting that I really didn't understand what it was all about or what we were supposed to be doing. It was particularly difficult for me to accept the idea that we seemed unable to define our task; the one thing I had thought I was certain about before joining the group was the notion that the group would set a task for itself as its first objective and then try to understand the process of group interaction involved in carrying out the task. As I came to understand that the task was not something outside the group, I was quite worried about the possibility that confronting each other with our honest feelings would be too painful or too dangerous. It was always easy for me to talk freely in the group, but I rather think now that any real expression of feeling on my part in the early sessions would have been extremely difficult or even impossible.

When the group leader confronted me with

the fact (and it was indeed a fact, although I had not recognized it as such) that I was engaged in a power struggle with him for direction of the group, I found it rather easy to accept his interpretation and to make a conscious decision to sit back for a while and try to find out what we were really supposed to be doing. From that time on, the group came into focus for me. I began to understand and to feel what was happening, and to take pleasure in being part of the experience. For one thing, I had gained some insight about my own style; for another, I began to enjoy the style of others in the group and to accept with some warmth and even tenderness the feelings displayed in our interaction.

What I found most engaging in our sessions and our weekend was the children and my new view of them. I discovered unsuspected depths of maternal feeling in myself, and I took enormous pleasure from the fact that the children responded warmly to me. There were moments when I felt like adopting the entire crew, oddly assorted as they were, and what I miss most now that the group is over is the continued intimate contact with the teenagers involved.

My feelings about the adults were more mixed. I came to feel a greater acceptance of the various individuals; while the group existed, I felt a genuine closeness to a number of people who at first had seemed unappealing or dull. There were even moments of real exhilaration in making emotional contact with some of the adults, but there isn't much carryover on that score. I don't really miss the adults as a group, although I find myself somewhat more tolerant of people in general than I was before our T-group.

And what has this left me with today, almost a year later? I think the effect has been profound, although I'm not sure just how to describe it. I've changed. I find it easier to express my feelings—not always, surely, but often enough so that I'm aware of a real difference from my pre-T-group self. I relate better to my own children, and to many of my students in school. There's a kind of ease in communication on the emotional level which I deeply enjoy. Again, I don't want to exaggerate the picture—I'm not a new me, and there are many times when I communicate poorly or not at all; but there are also many times when my emotional contact with people seems richer than it was before. And I do understand myself somewhat better, and can perceive more clearly how others react to me. Nor would I underestimate the fact that some enduring relationships, both with children and adults, emerged from the T-group, relationships which I cherish and would not have had without the T-group.

The parents of the children in the classroom encounter group had, of course, a wide variety of reactions. Since their children are sixteen- and seventeen-year-olds, adolescent rebellion is often in full cry with or without the group, and change in the teenagers is so rapid that attribution to any specific cause is difficult. Nevertheless, most of the parents were willing to comment on the situation from their standpoint.

They were asked to complete the sentence,

"Ever since the T-group, my child. . . ." Following are some representative responses.

Parents' reactions: . . . is more highly motivated, more communicative, more attentive in class, and a generally nicer guy to have around.

. . . is very happy. She has made many friends and found many new interests. She seems to understand other people and is very giving of herself. It helped my daughter to get a high self-esteem which made her very happy. She was more honest with herself and others. She is very expressive and full of enthusiasm.

. . . There was an unusual amount of stimulation for Joel—something which has been lacking in his contact with Hudson. I recommend this experience to all young people. It is marvelous to look into oneself at an early age and try to evaluate how you succeed or fail in learning processes and what is it that causes either—I'm still searching!

. . . seems more "open" and relaxed in himself, and in relationship with others.

. . . has become increasingly tolerant of others and their opinions. Prior, she had a tendency not to listen, to interrupt and be annoyed; now, find her listening more and more, wanting to hear your opinion. The T-group provided excitement in its novelty, an open approach and freshness, a broad scope of content not bound by curriculum, and additional motivation.

. . . shows greater interest in intellectual and creative activities. His friendships have also changed, from people who were non-achievers but having physical prowess, to those with a more searching and questioning turn of mind.

. . . is not particularly different. The impact of the T-group was somewhat noticeable at first, in terms of greater willingness to perceive other students' needs as people, but that appears to have worn off.

. . . is less inclined toward her school work, much less respectful toward her parents, much more self-centered. She has a definite "I know it all" attitude. The T-group has certainly not motivated her into more and better learning which, if I recall the statement of purpose prior to the formation of the group, was its prime intent. This was to be effected by breaking down personal barriers between pupil and pupil, and pupil and teacher. I see this year as almost a total waste academically. . . . I scarcely see any homework being done. I certainly see no maturation in self-discipline concerning work organization and habits and execution. I find her very much more difficult to cope with at home. She generally has to have the last word. What I call courtesy, thoughfulness, tact, considerateness, she conveniently calls duplicity. I feel engaging in this group process, which was supervised for three weeks, and practiced at every opportunity since then, has become a sport, a divertissement, a reason not to settle down to work.

. . . seems to be arrogant and quite the intellectual. This may or may not be because of the T-group experiment, but the change occurred at that time. He does seem to take more of an interest in world affairs and knows what he is talking about when he discusses them.

. . . had acted a little strange. She was tremendously enthusiastic at the start. As time wore on, she became a little difficult to live with. At times she was depressed and very sensitive. I liked her excitement with the project and her tremendous rapport with the entire group (at the start). She couldn't wait to go to school every day just so she could go to social studies. When the group started, my daughter was very outgoing. She also had a good opinion of herself. As time wore on, she became less sure of herself and started to doubt her acceptance by the group. She became afraid to participate. My daughter now has come full cycle and thinks it was a good thing.

The variety of responses reflects the different effects of the group on the students and also the variety of attitudes among the parents. Some parents seem bewildered by what had happened and can't understand the changing attitudes, as the one who is perturbed at the lack of homework and the accusation that her appeal to courtesy is called duplicity by her daughter. Not including the parents as members of the group is partly responsible for this, a failing commented on by this same parent who went on to say, "The T-group *must* be a combination of child and parent groups so that the child and parent might understand each other's problems. Once this is established I think we would have a solid foundation from which real maturity could spring."

This is an excellent example of how suggestions for next steps in an organizational project are generated by the preceding activities. From the parents' point of view, the overwhelming majority are excited, pleased, and stimulated by the results. But from a dissatisfied parent comes a proposal for making the experience even more effective by having a group of children and their parents together. By following along where needs arise, the organizational strains and inhibitions to growth can be met as they emerge, and suggestions for next steps can come from participants as well as staff.

The students were also asked to react to their experience. Following is a representative sampling of their responses.

Students' reactions: . . . A flame for the fuse leading to lasting relationships between me and others in the class. A suitable occasion for the sharing of my emotions. An opportunity to talk about my loves. A breaker of walls shielding the light shining in every individual in the class.

. . . An opportune time to let myself go without most of the restrictions existing in present-day situations.

. . . It is possible for me to use almost every adjective in "the book" in revealing the T-group's impact upon me. At times it was frightening, at others mildly interesting, and still others terrifically funny. My role ranged from active participant to casual observer. The experience has had its bad effects, but I see these as insignificant in the light of the insight that I gained through the many informal talks, which were such an important part of the whole operation. This insight (into others) made the entire experiment a success regardless of the negative aspects. In my role as a T-group member, I saw just how alike all people really were, regardless of religion or social background. Everyone had many of the same problems, whether domestic or otherwise, and many times their problems were more intense than my own. It was quite a shock indeed to find out how absurdly normal my life had been. This concept can be taught but it will only be *learned* through personal experience.

. . . For the past three weeks, I, as an individual, have experienced something quite unique. The T-group has significantly changed and eliminated many fears that I have had about myself as well as other human beings. A re-examination of my relationships with people of groups, and individuals, has proved to be most beneficial. By releasing my emotional fears and prejudices, and honestly expressing my feelings, I have come to regard myself as a more interesting and relaxed person. My honesty with myself as well as other people has left no room for nasty unsure feelings to distort themselves and corrode the channels of my mind so that I could emerge having an insecure, fearful, and unstable personality. Now, I feel a new sense of self. I feel as though I have just met what is inside of me, and most important of all, I like what I see, and I'm happy with the new "me."

. . . I don't expect that all my problems have been solved as a result of a mere three-week experiment. But what better way is there to start with the scrutiny and understanding of myself and my peers. To know what I really feel, who I really am, and why these things are so, is a most invaluable knowledge. Just watching the self-realization of other people has given me a sense of satisfaction and fulfillment. No longer do I succumb to the fear of rejection. I have found that if I speak my mind, and present myself as I really am, so much anxiety and hurt is eliminated. By learning to really communicate with myself and other people, I have found that life has become much more worthwhile. I have emerged with the insight that life does not always have to remain a painful struggle.

. . . The experiment was a success for those who wanted it to succeed. For those who wanted to remain in their own phony and unrealistic world it couldn't have been a great success.

. . . At first, action seemed forced and new to people in the group, which resulted in an extremely up-tight atmosphere. . . . As the days passed, the atmosphere in the group became one of easiness and of freedom. The atmosphere was as all classrooms should be . . . students should be eager to go to school. They should want to come and want to learn. School should not be a place to hate to go to. School should be as free and as pleasurable as possible. The happier the students, the more willing they will be to learn. The experiment is a step, the first noticeable step, towards this aim.

. . . looking back in retrospect, this has been one of the most unique experiences I've ever had, and I hope that I can profit by it.

Again, the variety is apparent in the students' responses. Another characteristic of these responses, especially as contrasted with the adults', is their frequent resort to creative expression such as poetry. The general freedom to explore and express themselves was much greater in the teen-agers than in the adults.

This project has been presented in some detail because it illustrates most of the issues involved in dealing with the impact of organizational factors on developing human potential. The targets of the training are students, teachers, administrators, and community members. The target areas are interpersonal relations, personal growth, and productivity. The institutions that are the objects of change are the school and the school community. In order to develop human potential many factors must be dealt with, including internal inhibitions built into people, both teenagers and adults, which prevent them from full expression; social constraints from peer groups; intergenerational conflicts; reconciliation of organizational factions, such as teacher groups, to allow them to facilitate rather than inhibit each other; integration of an established successful mode of behavior—in this case, teaching style, with newer methods capable of improving the old style; integration of new methods with an established system—in this case, the encounter group with the curriculum, to emerge with a more effective procedure.

For a social scientist entering an organization to help it become more supportive of the development of human potential, the greatest indication of his effectiveness probably comes when the members of the organization take over his objectives as their own. This is one reason why this project is so encouraging to me. All participants in the experiment—superintendent, parents, teachers, students—seem very involved with improving the curriculum, their relations with each other, themselves, and the whole school environment. Many are hard at work thinking, trying new ideas, relating to each other differently, trying new behavior. Ensuring that this type of vitality and inquiry continues after the intervener leaves requires establishing organizational structures backed by organizational commitment. In this school system, these structures are being evolved currently in the form of regularly scheduled encounter groups for teachers, regular cross-section groups, requests for funds to continue the project, formation of a joint committee to oversee and plan the program, and so on. When an organization includes as part of its ongoing activities the quest to be better far than you are, and combines it with the knowledge of how to use the latest techniques for such growth, the organization is indeed facilitating and enhancing joy.

Task Group Therapy

"Functional groups" from work organizations— people who work together—can also enhance the beneficial effect of the organization on human growth. A prime objective of these groups is to improve the working relations among co-workers. Functional groups are usually difficult to make work but very valuable if they go well. Three examples will illustrate the range of some of the valuable phenomena that can come from such groups.

A finance company that had been swindled of over a million dollars in a recent celebrated case decided that its credit department needed a thorough analysis. The author was asked to go away with the department—about twelve men— to a hotel, get a meeting room, close the door, and not come out for a week.

We did that, almost, with very salutary results. Starting with a great deal of guarded defensiveness, the atmosphere gradually softened and more openness was possible. From the discussions emerged the realization that the assistant manager of the department was doing almost all of the department's work. And for good reason. He knew much more about credit than anyone else, a fact acknowledged by all. However, he had difficulty delegating and developing younger men, with the result that he was overloaded and therefore less efficient.

After the dimensions of the situation were finally made clear, a process that took about three days, we took a look at the table of organization. At this point came the crucial role of the T-group discussions. The group now was capable of re-examining the organization, taking account of the personality and competence of the men, as well as the requirements of the job. The result was that another well-liked, less competent man was made another assistant manager in charge of allocating work so that the load could be distributed better. Further, the first vice-president, who was also acting branch head for all branches, agreed to train one man in each branch to take over as branch head within six months.

This solution took away from the original vice-president those things he did not do well—allocate work and train younger men—but allowed him to retain the functions he performed well—his own output and his training—and gave him sufficient time to do a good job. The new vice-president was strong in one weak area, allocating work, and could compensate. It is important that this solution was arrived at after lengthy and heated interchange, and the final solution was agreeable to all.

Thus, after the feelings were revealed—a process that usually takes a long time—it was possible to make a realistic assessment of the situation and arrive at a solution that improved the situation for everyone.

In a west-coast school district the superintendent had started an encounter group with the administrative personnel. After many months, openness began to increase. Over three years, several important principles emerged. One of these showed the mechanism of organizational inefficiency occurring through lack of interpersonal problem-resolution.

In one incident it was revealed that the music supervisor and the fifth-grade teacher did not get along well together, but they had arrived at a "civilized" solution to their problem. They treated each other very politely and tried to have as little contact as possible. This seemed very sensible until the consequences of this resolution were explored. When the fifth-grade classes studied geography they learned all about every country—except its music. In other words, the children paid the penalty for the inability of the music supervisor and the fifth-grade teacher to make a more productive resolution to their difficulties.

The discovery that the children were paying

for the inability of the adults to resolve their relational problems kept recurring: a new science program had been delayed three years because the science supervisor was ostracized by the teachers; children were overloaded with a double assignment because a principal couldn't resolve the conflict between the two teachers who advocated two different work units. And in one instance, the speech supervisor and the superintendent had generated some tension between them. Whenever there was a conference involving disposition of a child with a speech problem, the superintendent somehow forgot to include the speech supervisor. Thus, the one person best qualified to make a decision was never used. The encounter-group experience allowed the situations to be recognized, their consequences better understood, and a more satisfactory solution evolved.

Experience with a variety of organizations makes clear that this situation is by no means unique to this school system. In virtually every case failure to make a productive resolution of an interpersonal or organizational problem is paid for by someone, usually those lower in the hierarchy. This applies to parents' problems where children are the victims, and doctor-nurse difficulties paid for by patients, as well as teacher-friction burdening children. For the optimal atmosphere for developing human potential, other people and many parts of the organization must be kept in focus while more intensive work is being done on one particular functional unit.

One final example highlights another desirable outcome of a "task therapy group." In the Long Island project described earlier, another principle emerged from the twelfth-grade classroom encounter group which indicates a way toward improving learning.

During the latter stages of the group we were playing a game that involved identification of famous people from minimal clues. One clue was "V," and the answer was Churchill. "I don't get it," said one girl. "Whadda ya mean you don't get it," said another, "didn't you ever hear of V for Victory during the Second World War?!" "No I didn't. So what," was the weak defensive reply.

Later we analyzed this incident in the context of what it did to learning. The embarrassed girl revealed that she felt stupid and would probably never talk about World War II again. So the result of the interchange was to curtail seriously the participation and probably the learning of one class member. Why did this happen?

The attacker was very contrite and had to admit that she was probably trying to increase her own stature by putting down someone else. This led to a discussion of how everyone felt about his own competence, with other class members elaborating on these self-perceptions. The result was a decreased need to degrade each other. Then the discussion turned to the other side of the coin. How could class members not only not inhibit each other, but actually be helpful and facilitating? From whom did each person feel he could learn? Whom could he teach? We had turned the corner and had begun to explore the use of the organization—the class—as a facilitating device for the individuals within it. It is very difficult. It requires dealing with competition, jealousy, insecurity. And one day's discussion hardly resolved it for the students. But it helped some and led to some useful rumination on the part of the students.

Interracial Problems

A serious cultural block to self-realization is the prejudice against races, religions, sexes, and various other categories of people. Attempts to overcome prejudice have been prominent down through the ages. Success has been spotty but a few promising directions have emerged.

One is that the problem of overcoming prejudice allows for no simple solution. It is compounded of politics, economics, housing, labor, and interpersonal relations. Its solution must lie in intensive work at all levels.

Inferences derived from the intimacy hypothesis seem to offer the best hope for dealing with *feelings* of prejudice. This idea, supported by considerable evidence, asserts that such feelings are overcome through intimate contact with the targets of the prejudice. A man's racial prejudice, for example, is more likely to decrease if his immediate neighbor is a Negro, than if a Negro lives four doors away.

Several years ago, the Negro students of a major university asked the local YMCA to help improve communication among the races on the campus. The YMCA responded by asking several of us who were interested in this work to hold weekend retreats for this purpose. The results were fascinating.

On one such weekend, the author went to a

camp retreat with about twenty students, Caucasian, Negro, Oriental, about equal numbers of male and female. As usual, the start was slow, cautious, defensive. But as the time went on, gradually, people opened up. Once the students felt comfortable enough, the issues were raised and sharpened.

". . . What are your Negro stereotypes?" "You are dirty, stupid, fleshy, sexually promiscuous." "Yeh, well you, white boy, are exploitative, arrogant, and emotionally inhibited." And what happened after that exchange? Closeness. People began to talk to each other, to dance together, to explore one another as individuals. As one Negro put it, "I didn't lose my stereotypes of twenty years in one weekend, but once I've said them, they don't seem that important. The cards are on the table and we can look at each other as men, and go on from there."

". . . White liberals are just as bad as bigots, almost. They just accept everything I do instead of rejecting it. I could rape your sister and you wouldn't say a word, because I'm black. We don't want that. Know all the bad things about me too."

". . . It's not enough to say you treat us equally. How about getting to know me as a person? Building a relation!"

". . . You Negroes are always using your color to excuse everything. Why don't you get off the dime and do something instead of bellyaching?"

Then came an insight about motivation. Jews do very well in school. That's well-documented. Lately, Orientals have been challenging Jews scholastically. Negroes are usually low, understandably maybe, but low. White non-Jews run the gamut and average in the middle.

How about prejudice? Certainly the white non-Jews have the least directed against them, and the Negroes the most, by far. The Jews and Orientals are somewhere in between. Maybe some prejudice leads to a heightened motivation to perform. No prejudice raises the problem of motivation, which is then determined by many factors not related to prejudice, such as home life, intelligence, social status, etc. But overwhelming prejudice is crushing. Motivation is killed. Maybe, maybe not. But the weekend generated this thought. The participants were thinking creatively, out of their own experience, and thinking deeply.

There seems no question that this type of intimate contact frees people. The relations among many of the participants continued after the weekend. A small island of prejudice had been somewhat eroded. And it occurred in an organizational setting that supported the experience.

Family and Intimate Relations

One of the cornerstone institutions of our society is the family. Its importance in molding the individuals in the society can hardly be overestimated, but only recently has that importance been converted into a practical human technology. In the psychiatric realm, the recent emphasis on community and social psychiatry reflects the importance being placed on the family with mental illness. What good does it do to treat a patient and then send him back to the same home situation that got him in trouble?

So family therapy has developed. Skilled practitioners are now trained to deal with the family as a unit and to do therapy on the entire family social system. Changes may be needed in the whole family arrangement. Sometimes the improvement of the patient leads to a breakdown of the mother, or of a sibling. So all are dealt with together.

Gradually, examination of this area develops into an exploration of the whole field of marital relations. The institution of marriage is questioned. Is it successful? Is it the best pattern of intimate relations for everyone? What about close relations with people for short periods? Or relations that are renewed periodically? How can one learn to enjoy brief relations? They are far more frequent than lifelong relations, and yet there is little social support for learning to profit much from these contacts.

Groups that enter into this kind of thinking open up areas of vital importance to everyone. For some this is "thinking the unthinkable." For many more it is exciting to be able to ventilate and explore these feelings instead of hiding them and accumulating guilt. It is freeing. It is examining a social institution that can greatly enhance a person's self-realization, or that can—and perhaps this is more frequent—greatly inhibit his development. What is the effect two people have on each other in the intimacy of marriage? Is it growth-producing or destructive?

The investigation of organizational relations involves scrutinizing many of our sacred institutions, and it is often risky. If a company sends a man to a laboratory to understand himself better, he may, and sometimes does, come back and decide he's in the wrong line of work. When a Christian organization like the YMCA puts its boys through an encounter group to develop their independence and autonomy, they may find some of the boys questioning Christian principles. If an interracial workshop is formed to increase understanding, an interracial marriage may result. If students are made more autonomous through a group experience, they sometimes decide they don't want to learn about things of no importance to them. Or a married person in a workshop may be forced to acknowledge his real feelings of desperation and decide not to stay married. These are not only possibilities. They happen. They are necessary risks if organizational life is to be made supportive of individual development. We must stand ready for the conscientious questioning and examination of our social institutions. Despite its dangers we must "run where the brave dare not go." Only then can our society fully support the great effort forming to enhance the human potential.

6 · The Potential for Being More

Why do these methods work? What is the mechanism through which fantasy, dramatic, and non-verbal techniques bring about release and joy? Perhaps some speculations are in order.

First of all, to follow our notion that joy derives from realizing potential, what potential is it that these methods help the individual to realize? Perhaps it's the potential for being more of a person than I thought I could be; for being more significant, competent, and lovable; for being a more meaningful individual, capable of coping more effectively with the world and better able to give and receive love.

This possibility leads to a somewhat different emphasis in analyzing the requirements for growth than is usual in traditional psychotherapy. The problems that a person develops in growing up, that blunt the realization of his full potential, are not so much the objective events of his life as the feeling he gets about himself as an individual as a result of these events. For example, it is not so much a broken home that leaves its mark on a child, but his perception of his role in causing the situation, and of his ability to deal with it. If he is left feeling guilty, worthless, and helpless, these are the feelings which debilitate him. However, if he can feel guiltless, capable of functioning within the situation, improving it, compensating for its lacks, then the situation may induce a feeling of strength and confidence.

This notion takes on some credibility when the early childhood stories of severely disturbed psychotics are compared with those of successful business executives. In encounter groups I am frequently startled at the similarity of some of these childhood situations. Certainly they are not the same, but there are so many cases of successful executives whose father or mother committed suicide, who can't remember a happy moment in all their early years, whose parents were divorced or died very early, who were shifted from one orphanage to another throughout their entire childhood, who can never remember being kissed or even held by their parents, and so on. If these events occur in the lives of successful men, then there must be something more than traumatic childhood events that determine the direction of a child's evolution into a man.

Such analysis suggests that the place to concentrate for making useful changes in people is not so much on the traumatic historical events as on the individual's perception of himself. Perhaps this gives a clue to the effectiveness of fantasy, dramatic, and non-verbal methods.

The Don Quixote story is one of the most venerable and universally fascinating in all of world literature. From the recent stage production, *Man of La Mancha*, comes the song quoted at the beginning of this book. The lyrics suggest the connection of this universal story with the mechanism for increasing potential. "Dream the impossible dream," says Quixote, "fight the unbeatable foe," and be better far than you are.

In fantasy, the fantasizer has the experience of overcoming something he could not previously face. Rose finally destroyed the fearsome eyes, Sally built an impossible bridge to her heart, Nora deciphered her message, and Fran, after much struggle, finally destroyed her wall. All entered the fantasy situation feeling themselves incapable of these accomplishments, but through hard emotional labor, with outside support, they were able to attain their goals and feel their achievements with their whole being. They had dreamed the impossible dream. Their feeling about their ability to deal with the problem symbolized in the fantasy was very different after the fantasy. They perceived that their potential for being more was greater than they had thought, and this led to their feeling of exhilaration, strength, and contentment. Fran can now cope with heavy foods and be more open with people; Rose reports herself as "willing to try new things, to be with new people, to test myself more . . . I experience myself as having more guts and being less awed and less frightened by unfamiliar people and situations"; Sally was able to break out of her conflict about her marriage and her job and take definite action with which she feels comfortable; and Nora is ready to accept herself as an attractive person and to enter the competition with women and assert her femininity.

A similar thing can be said for the non-verbal experiences. Nancy physically broke out of her constriction; Tom was able to beat out the feelings he had thought he couldn't deal with;

Deborah went through the fearful meeting with her father and emerged strong and less guilty; John allowed himself to be lifted and Harold was bumped and they both found that they existed and that people cared. (John: "I guess for me the real impact of the exercise was being noticed, touched, and picked up. . . .") Evelyn swayed in front of the group and found that she wasn't wicked after all. They, too, report the feelings of renewal. Nancy says she can overcome the constricted feeling: "I've felt more feminine, more open, more spontaneous. I've done new things . . . I've made a couple of major decisions . . . I've done more things that I wanted to do"; Tom was able to confront his parents and really communicate his love; Deborah reports a much greater ability to deal with the problem of her father: "I would like to see him if I could, but I don't have that tension or anxiousness about it"; and John's improved feeling of significance is allowing him to take more chances. He reports, "I still feel some constraint in the use of my abilities, for fear this will alienate people. It is very true at work, but I am willing to risk this fear more."

And so it appears that these are methods to help us experience ourselves anew; to be able to cope more effectively with our feelings of unworthiness, ineptitude, coldness; and to come to accept, respect, and love ourselves more.

Perhaps we should join the Lord of La Mancha on what he calls his Quest—"to reach the unreachable star."

Epilogue

Joy is burgeoning. Methods for attaining more joy are growing and are becoming more effective. We are developing ways to make our bodies more alive, healthier, lighter, more flexible, stronger, less tired, more graceful, more integrated. We have ways for using our bodies better, for sensing more, for functioning more effectively, for developing skills and sensitivity, for being more imaginative and creative, and for feeling more and holding the feelings longer. More and more we can enjoy other people, learn to work and play with them, to love and fight with them, to touch them, to give and take with them, to be with them contentedly or to be happily alone, to lead or to follow them, to create with them. And our institutions, our organizations, the "establishment"— even these we are learning to use for our own joy. Our institutions can be improved, can be used to enhance and support individual growth, can be re-examined and redesigned to achieve the fullest measure of human realization. All these things are coming. None are here, but they are closer. Closer than ever before.

Ethan's feelings of fear and guilt are all over and he seems very absorbed sitting there by the window looking out at the night sky. Laurie and Caleb are lifting him up and Ethan is reaching out. Don't those kids know that the stars are un-reachable? No, I guess they don't. Wait—they all seem very joyful. What's that in Ethan's hand? Could it be . . . ?

William C. Schutz was educated at the University of California, Los Angeles, where he took his doctorate in psychology in 1951. After a year on the faculty at the University of Chicago Psychology Department, he conducted a research program in group social psychology while serving as an officer for the United States Navy.

At Harvard, from 1954 to 1958, he was a lecturer and research associate in the Department of Social Relations. He was research psychologist at the University of California, Berkeley, and a lecturer in psychiatry, School of Medicine, at the same university. As a consultant for several business corporations, he has advised on group behavioral problems and conducted small training groups for many public and private institutions, including the RAND Corporation.

Dr. Schutz is author of *FIRO: A Three Dimensional Theory of Interpersonal Behavior* (Rhinehart, 1958) and of numerous articles published in magazines, psychological journals, and books. He is Associate-in-Residence and a Director of the Residential Program, Esalen Institute, Big Sur, California.